COOKING THE SPANISH WAY

COOKING
THE SPANISH WAY

ELSA BEHRENS

SPRING BOOKS · LONDON

Contents

INTRODUCTION

I f you have opened this book, we are already friends. 'Cooking the Spanish Way'. What made you look at it? Have you been to Spain? and have you been left with a longing for a more intimate knowledge of that warm-hearted, colourful country? Or do you, perhaps, just hope to go there one day, and in the meantime you would like to find out what is in store for you in the way of food? No cups of tea and roast beef with Yorkshire pudding to be sure!

This book is a collection of dishes I have enjoyed during my twenty years' sojourn in Spain and, more recently, during my travels as a courier conducting tourists around. I will give you a culinary sample of just one week of our tour, and you will realise what a dramatic variation of characteristics and scenery awaits you. For, though this book only deals with the food of Spain, it proves once again that the cooking of a country reflects the life and the character of its people.

Olive oil, garlic, rice, pimentos, mussels and saffron are some of the ingredients that come to mind when thinking of Spain. Quite right - but many other things too, and it is a fallacy to believe that Spanish cooking need be heavier than French or Italian cooking. Only bad cooking is heavy, and food is only greasy if the oil is not treated in the correct way.

The ingredients should be put to fry when the oil is just beginning to smoke, and once the food is in the oil, the heat should be reduced so that the temperature is maintained. To cook the food too quickly would be to burn it on the outside, while it remains raw on the inside. Most Spanish cooks place a piece of bread in the oil to fry till golden, then take it out and the oil is ready for use; the bread has taken away any excess taste the oil may have had. Of course when food is fried in oil which is not sufficiently hot, it gets greasy and heavy. It is a proven fact that if olive oil is used correctly, the results are less greasy than frying with fat or lard, more commonly used in this country. However, a good cook will never strictly adhere to the rules of a cookery book once he or she is conversant with the ingredients. Most of the recipes in this book can be made with fat or lard instead of olive oil and all the ingredients are obtainable in this country - most of them in our own 'High Street', but certainly in the Spanish and Italian delicatessen stores, of which there are many all over the country and especially in London's Soho.

Though we are living in an age of frozen and canned foods, the interest in good and tasty cooking has never been as marked as it is today, and upon return from the sunshine and colour of our holidays, we can easily conjure up those brilliant carefree days again in our greyer clime. So let us embark upon our culinary tour and in the book you will find recipes for the dishes I mention.

We enter Spain by crossing the Pyrenees into the Basque country. Those sturdy Basques on the cool Atlantic coast give us strong fish dishes. So, when our car or coach stops in a little fonda near San Sebastian under the tamarisk trees, overlooking the sea, we sit down to our first Spanish meal - at a Spanish hour, for it is already two o'clock!

Entremeses
Bacalao a la Bilbaina
Cazuletas de Langostinos San Rafael
Coliflor al Gratin
Fruta y Queso

They give us no meat as it is Friday, and if you moan about your waistline and think it is a large meal - why, I have not ordered the entire menu - a Spaniard would have had an egg dish and a sweet besides!

Through woodland hills, along the banks of the Bidasoa river, past the paper mills and the green pastures of Navarre we go, and stop to have a drink in the little town of Vitoria. Then we enter the more austere plateaux of Castilla la Vieja, Old Castile. Our supper in the dining-room of our Burgos hotel is served by sturdy waitresses with beautiful faces under their starched white caps.

Melon con Jamón Serrano
Sopa Crema de Yema
Tournedo a la Crema con Patatas Fritas
Alcachofas con Salsa Tartara
Flan y Fruta

Next day, after visiting the Gothic Cathedral of Santa Maria, with the story of the national hero, the valiant Cid Campeador in our minds, we drive through rolling hills and dramatic isolation. Only from time to time we see little villages in the distance and a shepherd stands and gazes at us as we pass in a cloud of dust. We climb to the very top of the Somosierra Pass, and there we suddenly come upon a delightful Fonda, where they give us the following succulent meal:

Etremeses, comprised of
Albondigas, Buñuelitos de Queso, as well as the
   usual sardines, salads, etc.
Tortilla de Patatas
Ternera Rellena con Judias verdes
Crema de Chocolate
   and a nice hot coffee which
   is most welcome on this cold and
   misty summit

In the afternoon our road winds down through rocky mountains, past the Guardarrama range to the modern capital of Spain - Madrid. What a difference in temperature! It is hot, and that evening we are happy to sit on the roof garden of the hotel under the stars and dine to the strains of an old-fashioned quartet. The music is soothing and the food excellent.

Sopa Real
Huevos Cocotte a la Castellana
Tournedos a la Crema
Alcachofas al Gratin
Sabayon de Naranja

Next morning we take a day excursion to the ancient Moorish city of Toledo, once capital of Spain, and, after a morning's enthralling sightseeing, we go to a restaurant outside the old city walls and enjoy a truly typical meal:

Tomates Rellenos
Chuletas de Ternera a la Zingara
Esparragos Mimosa
Queso y Fruta

By the evening we are back in Madrid. Once again we sit on the roof garden, sipping Tio Pepe and talking about the wonderful El Grecos we have seen and the souvenirs we have bought, till they bring our supper:

Sopa de Queso
Camarones Fritos
Rosca de Carne con
   patatas y espinaca
Granizado de Café

In the morning we leave Madrid via Jetafe, the geographic centre of Spain. We lunch in the Government Parador, one of the motels which the Spanish Government have opened in that desolate and arid New Castile just for such as us, visitors using the highroads. It is delightfully cool inside and the dining room is large and shaded. They give us:

Canalones con Jamon
Chuletas de Cordero
   con patatas Vilareal
Queso y Fruta

We leave the Parador at Manzanares and drive through the valley of the Guadalquivir River and the increasing heat of Andalusia, past heavily laden little donkeys trotting for miles towards a distant little white-washed village where they are being anxiously awaited. We are very happy to find the 'patio' in our hotel in Córdoba cool, hung with flowers, and the dining room most colourful with its brilliantly-hued tiles. Here we start our supper with the cold and tasty Andalusian soup:

Gazpacho
Pastelitos de Pollo con Hojaldre
Escalopas de Ternera Rellenas
Legumbres variadas
Crema de Malaga

After a couple of days in Córdoba, the cultural centre of ancient Moorish Spain with its wonderful Mosque, we leave for Seville; it is not very far from Córdoba, so we arrive in time for lunch:

Pastel de Tortilla
Alcachofas a la Vinagreta
Fabada
Melocotones en Almibar

In the afternoon we wander through the narrow little streets and admire the flowers which we see in profusion in every window and every little patio. We drink Cinzano in a little wayside café. No licensing hours here! We enjoy a late dinner:

Trucha en aceite
Sopa de Tomate
Pastel de almendra
Arroz con Pollo

After two days in Seville we leave very early in the morning for Granada through miles and miles of olive groves, and suddenly in the evening light we see the Alhambra on the mountainside, with the Sierra Nevada mountains in the background. That fabulous Moorish Palace was the last stronghold of those strange, cultured people in Spain. Our hotel is on the mountain and we enjoy a lovely view while eating our last meal on this tour, for our six days are up. We continue towards the Mediterranean Coast through Cataluña and then through France. But your own personal culinary expedition to Spain is only just beginning - so HASTA LA VISTA! Till we meet again!

ELSA BEHRENS

Useful Facts and Figures

COMPARISON OF ENGLISH AND AMERICAN WEIGHTS AND MEASURES

English weights and measures have been used in most of the recipes in this book. The following table gives their conversions into cups and tablespoons. American cups are standard '½-pint' measuring cups, but the American pint is smaller than the British, and American half-pint cups are actually equivalent to $\frac{2}{5}$ of a British pint.

Liquid Measure

One pint of liquid may be regarded as equal to two American measuring cups for all practical purposes.

3 teaspoons equal 1 tablespoon

16 tablespoons equal 1 cup

Solid Measure

ENGLISH	AMERICAN
1 lb. Butter or other fat	2 cups
1 lb. Flour	4 cups
1 lb. Granulated or Castor Sugar	2 cups
1 lb. Brown (moist) Sugar	$2\frac{1}{3}$ cups
1 lb. Icing or Confectioner's Sugar	3 cups
1 lb. Syrup or Treacle	1 cups
1 lb. Dried Fruit	2 cups
1 lb. Chopped Meat (finely packed)	2 cups
1 lb. Lentils or Split Peas	2 cups
1 lb. Coffee (unground)	$2\frac{2}{3}$ cups
1 lb. Breadcrumbs	4 cups
½ oz. Flour	1 level tablespoon
1 oz. Flour	1 heaped tablespoon
1 oz. Syrup or Treacle	1 tablespoon
1 oz. Sugar	1 level tablespoon
1 oz. Jam or Jelly	1 level tablespoon
½ oz. Butter	1 tablespoon smoothed off

FRENCH MEASURES

It is difficult to convert to French measurements with absolute accuracy, since 1 oz. is equivalent to 28.352 grammes. The table below is therefore very approximate.

Liquid Measure

Approximately 1¾ pints may be regarded as equal to 1 litre. 1 demilitre is half a litre, and 1 décilitre is one-tenth of a litre.

Solid Measure

1 oz. is equal to approximately 30 grammes.
Approximately 2 lb. 3 oz. is equal to 1 kilogramme.

COOKING TEMPERATURES

Water

Simmering 180° F.
Boiling 212° F.

Oven Temperatures	Electricity °F	Gas Regulo No.
COOL	225—250	0—½
VERY SLOW	250—275	½—1
SLOW	275—300	1—2
VERY MODERATE	300—350	2—3
MODERATE	350—375	4
MODERATELY HOT	375—400	5
HOT	400—450	6—7
VERY HOT	450—500	8—9

Note. This table is an approximate guide only. Different makes of cooker vary and if you are in any doubt about the setting it is as well to refer to the manufacturer's temperature chart.

To convert °F. to °C., subtract 32° and multiply by $\frac{5}{9}$.
To convert °C. to °F., multiply by $\frac{9}{5}$ and add 32°.

The essential equipment for good Spanish cooking is more or less the same as for any good cooking. However, after studying these recipes you will realise that there is much more top-stove cooking than baking. That is because in the days when these recipes originated all the cooking was done on a charcoal stove and, incidentally, even the modern Spanish kitchen with all the latest equipment still has a charcoal stove in the corner, for dishes such as the Paella are best cooked in that way.

For Spanish cooking the following equipment is essential:

A large, heavy stock or soup pot with a close-fitting lid
An iron saucepan big enough to hold a chicken
A heavy-bottomed skillet or frying pan
A copper frying pan
A saucepan of quart size for quick boiling
A double-boiler (bain-marie)
A Paella or large, flat iron pan
Several baking or Pyrex dishes with covers
A mortar and pestle
A colander
A fine sieve
Several wooden spoons
A couple of china mixing bowls
A spirit of adventure - and last, but not least, patience!

HORS D'OEUVRE

Entremeses

Most Spanish meals begin with 'entremeses', many of which are tinned, such as sardines, tunny fish, button mushrooms, olives, etc. - but there are also a number of delicious little recipes for producing 'something different'.

Of course a considerable amount of preparation and a good deal of ingenuity are necessary to produce interesting and pleasing looking hors d'oeuvre. In the following pages we give a few suggestions for 'entremeses' as they are served in Spain.

TOMATES RELLENOS

Stuffed Tomatoes

For this take large, firm tomatoes. In Spain they are very often used while still green. Cut in half horizontally or just take off the top if they are not very large. Take out the soft centre pulp, leaving some of the hard flesh around the sides. Mix the pulp with chopped hard-boiled egg and chopped onion, or with anything left-over that is suitable. For instance, rice and chopped ham make a very delicious filling and can be served either hot or cold. A finely chopped salad makes a nice filling for tomatoes. When served cold, sprinkle with French salad dressing.

HUEVOS A LA RUSA

Russian Eggs

5 Servings

5 hard-boiled eggs	1 crisp lettuce
4 oz. chopped crab,	salt and pepper
shrimp or lobster	Savora mustard
½ cup mayonnaise	

These are simply stuffed hard-boiled eggs with special fish stuffing (either lobster, clam or shrimp). Cut the eggs in half and scoop out the yolk. Mix the finely chopped crab or shrimp, etc. with a thick mayonnaise and a little mustard and fill the eggs. Mash the yolks and sprinkle this over the top or make a bed of crisp lettuce leaves garnished with minced or mashed yolks and place the stuffed eggs on top.

HUEVOS EN SALSA AGRIA

Eggs in Sweet-Sour Sauce

6 Servings

6 eggs	1 tablespoon sugar
1 glass white wine	3 tablespoons vinegar
½ pint stock	butter or margarine
1 onion	1 tablespoon flour
bay leaf	salt and pepper
2 cloves	

Boil the eggs for 6 minutes and plunge into cold water to peel more easily. Melt the butter and simmer the chopped onion till soft; stir in flour and some salt and pepper till smooth and add the stock, cloves and bay leaf. Simmer for 15 minutes. Strain and reheat with the sugar and white wine. Put the eggs in the sauce and simmer for a few minutes. Garnish with fried bread croûtons and serve hot.

HUEVOS FARCI

Stuffed Hard-Boiled Eggs

Hard-boil as many eggs as required. Plunge into cold water and peel. Cut the eggs in half and carefully take out the yolk. Mash this up with finely chopped, sweet mustard pickle and fill the white again. Place on crisp green lettuce leaves.

AGUACATE CON CANGREJO

Crab in Avocado

4 Servings

1½ lb. fresh crab meat
juice of 1 lemon
3 sticks of celery chopped
½ cup French dressing

2 large ripe avocados
some crisp lettuce leaves
4 olives
cayenne pepper

Cut the avocados in half, lengthwise. Remove large stone. Carefully loosen meat from peel without breaking and sprinkle with lemon juice and salt to prevent discoloration.

In a separate bowl flake the crab meat, blend with salt and a dash of cayenne. Fill the avocado halves with crab mixture, chill, and when ready to serve place each avocado half on a bed of crisp lettuce leaves prepared on individual plates. Pour the French dressing over and garnish with an olive.

AGUACATE

Avocado Pear

Cut the avocado in half, take out the stone and place on a bed of crisp lettuce leaves. Garnish with grapefruit sections and serve with salad dressing (salt, pepper, vinegar and oil).

ALCACHOFAS CON JAMÓN

Artichokes with ham

Wash the artichokes, cut off the tops and soak in lemon water for 1 hour. Cook in salted boiling water till tender. Remove the leaves and take out the hearts, sprinkle with lemon juice end fill with a mixture of finely chopped ham and hard-boiled egg bound with mayonnaise. Serve chilled.

MELÓN CON TOCINO

Melon with bacon

Fry the bacon till crisp, take out of the fat and drain well, then curl around strips of melon. Fry little slices of bread in the bacon fat and drain. Serve the melon and bacon rolls on the fried bread. This dish is delicious both hot and cold. It is important to drain off the fat so it is not greasy.

CROQUETITAS DE CAMARONES

Little Shrimp Croquettes

5 Servings

1 lb. shrimps or prawns	1 tablespoon fresh
½ cup thick béchamel sauce	white breadcrumbs
(see page 186)	salt and pepper
2 egg yolks	nutmeg

Shell and clean the shrimps or prawns and chop up finely, mix with the béchamel sauce, the yolk of egg and the breadcrumbs, season with salt and pepper and a little nutmeg. Roll into tiny croquettes, baste in egg and breadcrumbs and deep fry. Serve hot on toothpicks as a cocktail savoury.

MELÓN CON JAMÓN SERRANO

Melon with Smoked Ham

4 Servings

This is a very popular dish during the melon season, which is the whole summer in Spain.

Cut a Honeydew melon in half, clean well of all pips and chill. When the moment to serve has arrived, cut into 8 slices, two for each person. Serve on individual plates with thin slices of smoked ham.

BOLITAS DE ORO

Golden Balls

4 Servings

8 eggs
1 cup mayonnaise
a little liver pâté
2 sticks celery

8 rounds of bread or toast
1 leaf gelatine
1 crisp head of lettuce
1 lemon

This is a very tasty hors d'oeuvre or egg dish and, if carefully made, looks very elegant.

Boil the eggs for exactly 10 minutes, plunge into cold water and peel. Cut the whites away very carefully, leaving the yolks whole. Place these on a flat dish. While the eggs are boiling, dissolve a leaf of gelatine in the mayonnaise. Pour some of this over the eggs and when it has slightly hardened, place the yolks onto the rounds of toast or bread, which have been spread with liver pâté and laid onto a bed of shredded lettuce and celery. In between the rounds place, rings of white of egg with some mayonnaise in the centre. Season the lettuce with salt, lemon and a little olive oil. Keep in cool place till served.

It Is 12 . 15

This name describes the dish of mixed hors d'oeuvre which is garnished to look like a clock.

In the centre of a large round dish put a rounded mound of potato salad, into which chopped ham, little peas and chopped olives have been mixed together with mayonnaise. Cut 6 hard-boiled eggs in half and place all around the edge of the salad like a clock. The figures of the clock can either be cut out of truffles and fixed to the egg with gelatine, or an easier and tasty way is to take a tube of anchovy paste and carefully press the paste out, making the face of the clock. The hands can be cut out of truffles or red peppers. Fix in the centre with a toothpick through a stoned olive. Garnish all around the dish with sliced radishes, olives and sliced tomato.

BUÑUELITOS DE JAMÓN

Little Ham Puffs

2 oz. flour	8 oz. finely chopped ham
2 eggs	salt and pepper
1 cup milk	olive oil

Separate the white from the yolks. Stiffly beat up whites. Mix the flour with the egg yolks, carefully so the paste is smooth. Fold in the whites, season and beat in the finely chopped ham. Drop a teaspoonful at a time into smoking hot oil. Drain well and serve either hot or cold as one of the many dishes of 'entremeses'.

BUÑUELITOS DE QUESO

Little Cheese Puffs

These are made in the same way as the Ham Puffs, but instead of chopped ham, add 8 oz. grated cheese.

ALBONDIGAS

Little Meat Balls

8 oz. minced meat	1 onion
2 oz. minced bacon	1 egg
1 clove garlic	1 cup breadcrumbs
oil for frying	salt and pepper

Chop the onion and garlic very finely and fry till golden. Drain well and mix with minced meat and minced bacon and half the egg beaten up, season and roll into small balls. Dip into rest of the egg and roll in breadcrumbs. Fry in deep hot oil. Strain and serve.

POMELOS CALIENTES CON CREMA

Hot Grapefruit With Cream

Cut the grapefruit in half, release the flesh from the skin and dust with brown sugar. Pour a little thick cream over each half and place in a hot oven for a few minutes. Serve hot.

APIO RELLENO

Stuffed Celery

Take a large fresh celery, separate each stick, wash and scrape till white. Cut into pieces about 2 inches long and fill with soft cream cheese. Sprinkle with cayenne.

CANAPES CALIENTES DE QUESO Y JAMÓN

Hot Cheese and Ham Canapés

white bread	olive oil
butter	salt and pepper
2 egg yolks	1 teaspoon mustard
creamy cheese	slices of smoked ham
juice of ½ lemon	

Cut thick slices of white bread into rounds with a glass, butter and toast lightly.

Prepare a hot mayonnaise by beating up the yolks with a metal whisk in a double saucepan (bain-marie). Continue to beat while gradually adding the olive oil till the sauce thickens. Take off the fire, add salt and pepper, mustard and lemon juice to taste, beating up well all the time. Spread the mayonnaise onto the buttered toast and on this lay a slice of ham. Spread with cheese and put into a hot oven for a few minutes. Serve hot.

DELICIAS CON QUESO

Cheese Patties

6 egg whites	breadcrumbs
4 oz. grated cheese (either Gruyère or Cheshire)	1 egg yolk butter or oil for frying

Beat the egg whites till stiff snow. Fold in the grated cheese and beat. Season and roll into small balls or croquettes, dip into breadcrumbs, then into the beaten yolk and again into the breadcrumbs. Deep fry in oil or butter and serve very hot. (If butter is used for frying it is wise to put in a drop of oil to prevent burning.)

DELICIAS A LA PIGNATELLI

Almond Patties

Exactly as above, but instead of cheese, fold in ground almonds or coconut.

Chicken Filling

Instead of cheese, left-over chicken and chicken livers can be used.

1 oz. butter	$\frac{1}{2}$ pint milk
2 oz. flour	salt and pepper
	nutmeg

Mince the chicken, chicken livers and if available a little ham. Melt the butter and add the flour, stirring to a smooth paste. Gradually add the milk, stirring all the time. Season and add the minced chicken, etc. till sufficiently thick to fill the patties. Fill and heat before serving.

Lobster Filling

As above, with minced lobster instead of chicken.

Mushroom Filling

As above, with chopped mushrooms.

QUESO CON NUECES

Cheese With Nuts

American cheese   ketchup
mustard   walnuts

Make a paste with the cheese, mustard and ketchup over a low fire. Put a little between two walnut halves, thus sticking them together.

CIRUELAS RELLENAS

Stuffed Prunes

prunes   1 egg
ham   breadcrumbs
oil for frying   toothpicks

Leave the dried prunes in water for 1 hour, dry well and remove the stone without breaking the prune too much. Fill with chopped ham and dip in beaten egg and breadcrumbs. Fry in deep, hot oil, drain well and serve hot on toothpicks.

TRUCHA EN ACEITE

Trout in Oil

trout onions
olive oil vinegar
bouquet of herbs bay leaf

Fry the trout in olive oil with the herbs and finely sliced onions until tender. Put into a porcelain bowl, cover with vinegar and a bay leaf, leave for 4 or 5 days. At the end of that time it will be delicious for hors d'oeuvre.

ARENQUE LUCAS

Smoked Herring with Mayonnaise

Leave the smoked herring in milk overnight. This makes it less salty. Throw the milk away and serve with mayonnaise, sprinkled with chopped hard-boiled egg and cucumber.

Sopas

At least one Spanish meal a day starts with soup. Sometimes this is the main dish, but whether consommé or thick soup, the basis is always good, well-flavoured stock, such as peasants have in the mountainous regions of Spain, where many of the dishes are 'cocidos', put to cook in a big iron cauldron over the coal fire, while the family is working in the fields, or has gone to sell their wares in the distant markets. Water often has to be fetched from a far-off well, so in those humble homes there is usually a stock-pot to hand, on which the soups and stews are based. But even if we have no stock-pot ready when we need it, fresh stock is easy to make.

To make brown stock, take a shin of beef in the proportion of 1 lb. meat to each quart of water with plenty of fresh vegetables.

For bone stock, boil the bones for at least 5 hours.

Vegetable stock is good with 1 lb. of fresh vegetables to 1 quart water. Cook for at least 1 hour.

The water in which fish is boiled makes good fish stock.

Keep the stock or soup clear of grease by skimming when it comes to the boil. When making a thick soup, see that the binding is well cooked and keep smooth.

CONSOMME SENCILLO

Clear Consommé

6 Servings

2 lb. lean boiling beef	2—3 carrots
2 veal bones	1 onion
1 large turnip	4 pints water
a sprig of parsley	salt and pepper

Cut the meat into small pieces, wash and cut up the vegetables. Put everything together with the bones into a large casserole, add 3 pints of cold water and bring to a boil. Take the scum off the top, add salt and pepper and simmer slowly for about 3 hours. Strain the liquid, which can be used as clear soup (add a little dry sherry to improve the taste) or as stock for more elaborate soups.

SOPA REAL

Royal Soup

4 Servings

4 oz. smoked ham	3 pints stock or if water
1 cooked breast of chicken	is used 8 Maggi or Oxo cubes
3 hard-boiled eggs	salt and pepper
1 wine glass sherry	

Chop up the chicken and ham very fine and also the hard-boiled egg, put into the warmed soup tureen, pour the hot soup over it and serve with fried bread croûtons. If Maggi or Oxo cubes are used instead of stock, dissolve the cubes in a cup of boiling water, add the rest of the boiling water and almost bring to boil, but not quite.

SOPA CATALANA

Catalan Soup

4 Servings

3 large onions	2 oz. chopped ham or bacon
1 glass white wine	2 egg yolks
1 stick celery	3 pints stock or water
3 tomatoes	thyme and parsley
3 potatoes	a pinch of nutmeg

Slice the onions and fry in olive oil or bacon fat till golden in the casserole in which you are going to make the soup. Stir to prevent catching and add the diced ham or bacon, then the tomatoes, cut in quarters, and the chopped celery. After a few minutes pour in the glass of wine, let it almost come to the boil and then add the stock or water. Finally put in the finely diced potatoes and season.

UN BUEN CALDO GALLEGO

Gallego Soup

6 Servings

8 oz. white beans	8 oz. boiling beef
knuckle bone bacon	1 white cabbage
veal bone	3—4 potatoes
	salt and pepper

This is a nourishing, strong soup for a cold day. Soak beans overnight in cold water. Put 7 pints water to boil in a large saucepan, add beans, bacon and veal bones and minced beef. Bring the to boil and take off the scum, then simmer for 2—3 hours. Add shredded cabbage and diced potatoes, season to taste, remove bones and serve.

ESCUDELLA A LA CATALANA

Catalan Thick Soup

4 Servings

1 lb. potatoes	4 oz. bacon
4 oz. rice	1 onion
4 oz. short, thick spaghetti	2 carrots
small piece cabbage	2 turnips
garlic clove	1 stick celery
saffron	2½ pints stock

Wash and cut the vegetables into small pieces, boil in the stock for 30 minutes. Add the chopped bacon, the rice and the spaghetti. Mix the saffron with a little of the stock and add. Boil for another 10—15 minutes. Season to taste and serve.

SOPA DE MENUDOS

Giblet Soup

4 Servings

1 pint stock	any chicken giblets or left-overs
2 eggs	of meat, ham, chicken or turkey

Add the boiled giblets or left-over meat, finely chopped, to the stock and simmer for a few minutes. Separate the yolks from the whites of the eggs. Beat up the yolks and beat into the stock and then do likewise with the whites. Season to taste and serve in cups or bowls.

PUREE LEONTINO

Thick Vegetable Soup

6 Servings

2 lb. leeks	1 tablespoon chopped parsley
1 onion	1 tablespoon chopped mint
1 cup spinach	1 tablespoon chopped celery
1 cup green peas	¼ pint olive oil
1 cup shredded lettuce	lemon juice
½ pint milk	salt and pepper

Wash and cut the leeks into slices. Into a large casserole put
the olive oil and when it is warm put in the leeks, seasoned
with salt and pepper and the juice of a lemon. Simmer slowly
for about 20 minutes. Now add the chopped spinach, the
peas and the lettuce, stir a minute or two and add a quart of
water or stock. Cook until the vegetables are soft - about
10 minutes, then pass through a sieve. Add the milk to the
purée and stir in the finely chopped parsley, mint and celery.
Re-heat gently. Fry some croûtons of bread and serve with
this delicious green soup.

SOPA DE QUESO

Cheese Soup

4 Servings

1 oz. fat
2 oz. butter
4 slices white bread
1 onion

1 cup grated cheese
1 pint stock or water
salt and pepper
a pinch of nutmeg

Remove crusts from slices of bread. Heat the butter and fat in a pan and cook the finely chopped onion till tender. Put 2 slices of white bread in a saucepan, over this pour half of the fat and the onions from the pan, over this sprinkle half the grated cheese, repeat this: two slices of bread, the rest of the fat and onions and the rest of the cheese. Season and pour in the stock. Simmer or put into the oven till the bread has dissolved. This is a tasty, thick soup.

SOPA CREMA DE YEMAS

Egg Cream Soup

8 Servings

4 pints consommé
¼ pint cream

6 egg yolks
4 tablespoons chopped ham or chicken

Separate the yolks, taking care that no white remains. Beat the yolks up well, add the cream and heat together. Add the stock and cook slowly in double saucepan (bain-marie) beating all the while. When the soup starts to thicken add salt and pepper. Pour through a sieve straight into a heated tureen. Add chopped ham or chicken or fried bread croûtons.

SOPA DE AJO A LA CASTELLANA

Garlic Soup Castilian Style

4 Servings

2 garlic cloves	2 tablespoons olive oil
4 slices white bread	salt and pepper

This very tasty soup is made in every Spanish household, both rich and poor. It is made with practically nothing and is consequently not very nourishing, but for many poor families it means 'something in their stomach'.

Remove crusts from bread. Pound the garlic cloves and fry in oil. When they are golden add the bread and fry slightly, season and pour into 2 pints cold water. Bring to the boil and continue to boil for about 10 minutes.

SOPA DE AJO CON HUEVOS

Garlic Soup with Egg

Make a garlic soup as above, but when frying the bread, add 4 tomatoes and fry, then add to water and boil in the usual way. Just before serving beat up the yolks of 3 eggs and add to the soup.

[38]

POTAJE DE GARBANZOS Y ESPINACAS
A LA ESPAÑOLA

Spanish Pea and Spinach Soup

4 Servings

1 lb. chick peas	1 carrot
olive oil	1 bouquet herbs (bay leaf,
2 onions	parsley etc.)
small piece of dried cod	1 clove garlic
4 oz. spinach purée	2 tomatoes
parsley	

Soak the chick peas in cold water overnight. Then put them
into a large saucepan of boiling water, add a tablespoon of
olive oil, 1 onion, carrot, garlic and herbs and the small
piece of dried cod. Boil till the chick peas are tender (about
1½ hours). Pass the whole thing through a sieve and add
cooked spinach purée. Put on one side while frying the other
onion, chopped, the garlic clove and a little chopped parsley.
Add a little of the soup, simmer for a moment and add to
the rest of the soup. Continue to simmer for another 45 minutes. A chopped boiled egg can be added if required.

It is important that this soup should be nice and creamy
without being too thick, which would make it stodgy.

POTAJE DE HABICHUELAS ALFONSINAS

Broad Bean Soup Alfonsina

4 Servings

8 oz. white or broad beans
2 garlic cloves
1 onion
2 tomatoes

4 oz. Butifarra (boiling
     sausage)
1 hard-boiled egg
3 pints water

Soak the beans in cold water for several hours and boil. Into
a saucepan pour some olive oil and heat, cook the garlic,
chopped onion and tomato, add the Butifarra and the beans,
which have been drained (keep the water) fry altogether
slightly and add the water from the beans. Boil for a few
minutes and when ready to serve add the chopped hard-
boiled egg.

SOPA DE CEBOLLA

Onion Soup

4 Servings

2 pints stock
4 onions
1 egg yolk

2 potatoes
olive oil
salt and pepper

Boil the diced potatoes in the stock till tender. Meanwhile,
fry the chopped onions in a little oil till golden. Add to stock
and continue to boil for 15 minutes, pass through a sieve and
return to saucepan. Season to taste and add a beaten egg
yolk. Serve immediately.

SOPA AL CUARTO DE HORA

The Quarter of an Hour Soup

4 Servings

8 clams	1 tin small peas (*petits pois*)
8 shrimps (peeled)	a dash of saffron
2 hard-boiled eggs	2 pints stock
4 oz. chopped ham	4 oz. white fish (cod or turbot etc.)
6 oz. rice	salt and pepper

This is a good meal in itself. Boil the clams until they open; keep the water and add to stock, bringing it up to required quantity. Take the clams out of their shells and return to boiling stock. Cut the white fish to small pieces and add together with the rice, chopped ham and chopped hard-boiled egg. Meanwhile pound the shrimps in a mortar with the saffron, salt and pepper and add. In a quarter of an hour it will be a delicious soup.

PERLAS DORADAS

Golden Pearls

6 Servings

3 pints stock	3 heaped tablespoons tapioca
2 egg yolks	salt and pepper

Into boiling stock slowly pour the tapioca, cook for 10 minutes, stirring all the time to prevent lumps from forming. Beat the egg yolks into the soup and serve with fried croûtons.

SOPA CON JAMÓN

Soup with Ham

6 Servings

4 pints stock	1 egg
6 teaspoons tapioca	1 cup chopped ham

To the boiling stock gradually add the tapioca, stirring so it does not lump. Simmer until tapioca is tender. Beat up an egg and add, stirring all the time. Simmer for 1 minute and add the ham. Season to taste and serve immediately.

GAZPACHO

Cold Soup As Made In Andalusia

4 Servings

There are many ways of making this refreshing cold soup but the result is always delicious.

For those who are fortunate enough to have a mixing machine here is a good recipe:

2 lb. tomatoes	2 tablespoons oil
1 onion	2 tablespoons vinegar
1 clove garlic	salt and pepper
2 pimentos	

Wash the tomatoes, peel the onions, wash the lemon and cut in half to extract the pips. Clean the pimentos of all the inner seeds. Put all this in the mixing machine with the oil and vinegar. Season to taste with salt and pepper and a pinch of sugar. Put in the refrigerator to cool.

Serve with finely diced cucumber, tiny pieces of white bread or toast and finely chopped onion.

A Simple Gazpacho

1 tin tomato juice	2 tablespoons vinegar
1 lemon	salt and pepper
2 tablespoons oil	

Mix this well, cool in the refrigerator and serve with finely diced pimentos, onions, cucumber and bread.

SOPA DE VIGILIA

Soup For Friday

6 Servings

3 pints water or fish stock	2 tomatoes
8 oz. fresh cod	1 small cauliflour
1 onion	$\frac{1}{2}$ cup rice
1 clove garlic	salt and pepper
1 slice white bread	oil for frying

Fry the sliced onion, garlic and fish in oil, till tender, add a slice of white bread and fry, last of all add the tomatoes. Drain off the oil and put into boiling water or fish stock, cut the cauliflower into little pieces and boil till tender. Pass the whole through a sieve and add the boiled rice or croûtons. Serve hot.

SOPA PURÉ DE PATATAS Y ZANAHORIAS

Potato and Carrot Purée

4 Servings

2 onions	4 potatoes
2 carrots	salt and pepper
2 leeks	white bread for croûtons
bay leaf	butter or oil for frying

Fry chopped onions, carrots, leeks and a bay leaf in butter, add diced potatoes and pour in the stock. Simmer over a low fire. When tender pass through a sieve into another saucepan. If the purée is too thick, add a little milk or stock. Season to taste and serve with fried croûtons.

PORRU - SALDA

Basque Soup

4 to 5 Servings

2 lb. dried cod	2 teaspoons oil
3 leeks	1 garlic clove
3 potatoes	salt and pepper

Soak the cod overnight, put to boil in cold water with an onion for about 15 minutes. Flake the cod with a fork. In the meanwhile fry the garlic and the leeks in a little oil, and the peeled, diced potatoes. Add the cod and simmer, mix a little of the fish stock and bring to boil. Mash everything up together, slowly adding the rest of the fish stock. Simmer for an hour and serve hot.

CREMA DE LANGOSTINOS

Cream of Lobster Soup

5 Servings

4 oz. lobster, prawns or shrimps
4 oz. butter
2 oz. ground rice

2 pints milk
2 tablespoons cream
1 liqueur glass cognac or sherry
salt and cayenne pepper

Cook the lobster or shrimps in boiling water and salt. Keep the water. Take off the claws, tails, etc. and pound part of the meat well in a mortar. Mix this together with the ground rice and make a smooth paste with a little cold milk and butter.

Simmer slowly, stirring well with a wooden spoon. Take off the fire and pass through a sieve. Put the lobster cream into the casserole with the rest of the lobster or shrimp meat, adding sufficient of the stock and milk to make a creamy soup, simmer, add the sherry and just before serving stir in the cream and a little cayenne pepper.

Huevos

Egg dishes are always an excellent stand-by and with a little imagination they can be garnished so as to become the main dish.

The secret of a good omelette is to have the pan really hot before you put in the butter and to have the butter really hot (but not brown) before you put in the eggs. For a light omelette beat the eggs up well and for an extra light one, beat the whites apart and fold in. A few drops of water added to the eggs are preferable to milk, which tends to make the omelette stodgy. The difference between a French omelette and a Spanish omelette is that the French omelette is underdone on the inside and folded over, while the Spanish omelette remains round and

[47]

flat and is done well on both sides. To avoid turning over, the top can be finished off under the grill.

HUEVOS FRITOS AL BUÑUELO

Eggs fried like fritters

Melt some butter or margarine in a deep-frying pan. Break the egg into the very hot butter, hold the pan slanting sideways so the butter covers the egg and the white is wrapped over the yolk so there is no yolk showing. Fry well on both sides and serve with white rice.

HUEVOS ESCONDIDOS

Hidden Eggs

4 Servings

Make four, fine, large pancakes. Scramble 6 eggs in the usual way and divide into four portions. Wrap the scrambled egg into slices of ham, and roll and enclose the ham roll in a pancake. This makes a delicious luncheon dish or a first course for dinner.

HUEVOS EMPANADOS

Eggs in Breadcrumbs

6 Servings

7 eggs
breadcrumbs

oil or butter for frying
tomato sauce

Poach 6 eggs and carefully cut the white to make them even
and round; dip into breadcrumbs. Beat up 1 egg and dip the
eggs into this and then again into the breadcrumbs. Salt and
fry in butter or oil till golden.

Serve with a thick tomato sauce, prepared with tomato
purée and a dash of sherry.

TORTILLA DE PATATAS A LA ESPAÑOLA

Spanish Potato Omelette

3 or 4 Servings

6 eggs
1 onion
salt and pepper

1 lb. potatoes
oil for frying

Chop up the onion and fry till golden. Peel and dice the
potatoes. Slowly fry these till tender, but not crisp (boiled
potatoes can also be used).

Beat the eggs up well with a few drops of water. Take care
not to leave too much oil in the pan. Place the potatoes and
onion in and pour the eggs over. When done on one side,
carefully turn over by slipping onto a saucepan lid and
putting a little more oil into the pan, return to pan. Serve
immediately.

All Spanish omelettes are served flat, not rolled over like
a French omelette.

TORTILLA MADRILEÑA

Madrid Omelette

4 Servings

3 sweetbreads
6 eggs
2 onions
8 oz. butter
2 tomatoes or small tin
of tomatoes

4 oz. chopped ham
1 glass dry sherry or
white wine
chopped parsley
salt and pepper

Fry 1 chopped onion in butter; before it turns colour add the
sweetbreads, a little chopped parsley and when almost done
add the sherry or white wine. Keep warm while making the
omelette. Fry 1 finely chopped onion in butter; as soon as it
starts to turn golden add the chopped ham and 6 eggs well
beaten up. Season and make a flat round omelette, cook on
both sides. Place on serving dish and garnish with the sweet-
bread and fried tomatoes.

TORTILLA DE RIÑONES

Kidney Omelette

4 Servings

The same as above, only with kidneys instead of sweetbreads.

HUEVOS A LA FLAMENCA

Eggs Flamenca Style

6 Servings

6 eggs (or 2 each if required)	4 oz. chopped ham
2 lb. tomatoes	4 oz. chorizo (garlic sausage)
8 oz. small peas (*petits pois*)	1 onion
8 oz. green beans	2 garlic cloves
8 oz. asparagus tips	1 teaspoon chopped parsley
olive oil	$\frac{1}{2}$ pint stock
6 slices ham	3 sweet peppers (tinned)
salt and pepper	a dash of sugar

Heat the oil in a saucepan and slightly fry the onion and garlic, but do not allow to brown, add the chopped ham, the pepper and the tomatoes cut into slices, season with salt and pepper and a dash of sugar (the latter to modify the acidity of the tomatoes). Add the stock (or water), cut into small pieces and add the green beans and the peas. (If tinned *petits pois* are used do not add till everything else is tender. This also applies to asparagus tips.) Cook slowly, till tender.

Place the cooked vegetables in a baking dish, break the eggs over them, spacing them well, garnish with the chorizo and strips of ham and tinned red peppers. Place at the bottom of a hot oven so the whites set quickly, leaving the yolks liquid. Serve immediately with strips of fried bread. The Huevos Flamenco are suitable for little individual dishes.

HUEVOS PRESIDENCIA

Presidential Eggs

6 Servings

6 eggs	$\frac{1}{2}$ cup flour
4 oz. liver pâté	$\frac{1}{2}$ pint milk
1 lb. chopped spinach	salt and pepper

Hard-boil 6 eggs, plunge in cold water and peel. Cut in half and take out the yolks; mix these with the liver pâté and replace in the white halves. Keep in a warm place till the spinach is boiled and strained. Line a dish with the spinach to make a nest for the eggs; then make a béchamel sauce with the yolk of an egg, flour and milk (see p. 186) and pour over the eggs. Heat quickly in the oven and serve immediately.

HUEVOS EN SORPRESA

Surprise Eggs

6 Servings

6 eggs	a Maggi cube
8 oz. mushrooms	chopped parsley
(or mushroom stalks)	bread crumbs
4 oz. butter	salt and pepper
3 chicken livers	

Slice the mushrooms and livers and fry gently in a little butter. Pour into a baking dish. Over this open the eggs carefully so they do not break. Over the eggs sprinkle 2 teaspoons of water in which the Maggi cube has been dissolved. Dust with bread crumbs and chopped parsley. Bake in hot oven till the whites have set. Care must be taken not to allow the yolks to harden. Serve immediately.

HUEVOS CUBANOS

Cuban Eggs

6 Servings

2 large cups plain boiled rice	4 bananas
4 eggs	1 tablespoon flour
olive oil	salt and pepper

Prepare a nest of rice in 4 individual dishes, keep hot till required. In plenty of hot oil, fry the eggs, folding the whites over the yolk and turning so that they are fried on both sides, drain well and place on rice.

Cut the bananas in two, roll in flour and fry for 2 minutes, place a piece on each side of the egg and serve immediately.

HUEVOS FRITOS A LA ANDALUZA

Fried Eggs Andalusian Style

Fry the eggs as above on both sides, serve with fried garlic sausage and fried potatoes.

HUEVOS RANCHERO

Eggs Ranchero Style

4 Servings

4 oz. minced meat   olive oil
1 onion   1 small tin tomato purée
4 eggs   2 large cups plain boiled rice

Fry the chopped onion together with the mincemeat. When brown add the tomato purée, slightly diluted with water; simmer till the eggs are fried in the ordinary way. Line 4 individual dishes with rice, place the fried egg in the centre and over it the meat and tomato sauce. Serve immediately.

HUEVOS COCOTTE A LA CASTELLANA

Castilian Eggs in Cocotte

6 Servings

6 eggs   2 tablespoons grated cheese
4 oz. minced meat   1 onion
2 cups béchamel sauce   olive oil
  (see p. 186)

The eggs should be very fresh for this dish. Fry the chopped onion, add the minced meat and fry till brown. Line the individual baking dishes with a drop of oil and the minced meat. Onto this carefully break an egg. Put into hot oven till the white has set, then add the béchamel sauce. Sprinkle with grated cheese and replace in oven for a couple of minutes. Serve immediately.

HUEVOS REVUELTOS AL PISTO

Scrambled Eggs with Vegetables

4 Servings

2 or 3 small marrows
3 pimentos (sweet peppers)
8 oz. tomatoes
4 oz. chopped ham
1 onion

2 diced, boiled potatoes
1 garlic clove
8 eggs
oil
salt and pepper

Peel the tomatoes and cut, peel and cut the marrows and the peppers into small squares. Heat the oil and fry the onion and garlic till golden, then add the tomatoes and peppers. when these are tender add the potatoes, last of all add the chopped ham, season with salt and a pinch of sugar. Keep warm till required. Beat the eggs up well and scramble. Serve together with the fried vegetables called 'Pisto'.

HUEVOS EN CAMISA

Eggs in Shirts

as many eggs as required
butter

a little parsley
salt and pepper

Grease a baking dish well with butter. Separate the yolks from the whites of the eggs. Place the yolks in a greased dish. Beat up the whites till stiff, adding a little finely chopped parsley or grated cheese. Cover the yolks and bake for 5 minutes. This very easy and quick dish is delicious.

CONCHAS DE HUEVO A LA FLORENTINA

Scrambled Eggs Florentine Style in Shells

4 Servings

6 eggs	1 lb. spinach
1 yolk	4 oz. butter
4 oz. grated Parmesan	3 tablespoons milk
or Gruyère Cheese	nutmeg
salt and pepper	

Boil the spinach (a packet of frozen spinach can be used) chop well and pass through a sieve and season. The spinach purée should be quite dry. Add the beaten-up yolk, a teaspoon of butter and beat up well.

Have 4 shells or little dishes ready. Put the purée all around the border, leaving the centre free for the scrambled eggs. To scramble, melt a little butter in a pan, when hot, pour in the beaten eggs, stirring all the time, add the grated cheese and the milk, season and continue to beat till the eggs are firm and creamy. Immediately put inside the circle of spinach. Sprinkle with cheese and serve hot.

HUEVOS ESCALFADOS A LA ESPAÑOLA

Spanish Poached Eggs

6 Servings

6 eggs	1 small marrow
2 onions	olive oil
4 tomatoes	1 clove garlic
2 pimentos	salt and pepper
	a dash of sugar

Chop the onion, peel and chop the tomatoes and pimentos (taking care to extract the seeds) also peel and chop the marrow. Heat the oil and fry the onion and garlic till golden, then add the pimentos and marrow and finally the tomatoes, salt and pepper. Add a dash of sugar. Fry till quite tender. Line a baking dish or individual little dishes with this. Place the poached eggs on top, garnish with small triangles of bread, fried crisp in oil.

HUEVOS FRITOS A LA ESPAÑOLA

Spanish Fried Eggs

6 Servings

Exactly as above, only fry instead of poaching the eggs.

HUEVOS REVUELTOS A LA ESPAÑOLA

Spanish Scrambled Eggs

6 Servings

As above, with scrambled eggs.

HUEVOS AL PLATO AL PARABERE

Fried Eggs Parabere

3 Servings

6 eggs	1 small packet frozen spinach
4 oz. Salami type sausage	butter or margarine for frying
4 onions	

Finely chop the onions and simmer till tender, add 6 slices
of sausage. Line individual dishes with sausage, sprinkle the
onion over and break 2 eggs over this bed and fry. In the
meanwhile boil and cream the spinach, pass through a sieve.
When the eggs are done, circle with spinach and serve fried
croûtons. To make this dish richer a little béchamel can be
poured over the eggs.

PASTEL DE TORTILLAS ESPECIAL

Special Omelette Cake

4 Servings

8 eggs
4 oz. mushrooms (or
  mushroom stalks)
4 oz. shrimps
2 cooked potatoes
fresh tomato sauce

4 oz. mixed cooked vegetables
  (*petits pois* and carrots)
1 onion
fat or oil for frying
salt and pepper

Dice the mushrooms, shrimps, potatoes and mixed vegetables separately. The dish is composed of four small, round omelettes of 2 eggs each - one mushroom, one shrimp, one potato, and one mixed vegetable placed one on top of the other and garnished with tomato sauce. When serving, cut like a cake and the different colours and tasteds blend to make an outstandingly attractive dish.

TORTILLA A LA ÚLTIMA

Omelette in the Latest Style

Make a French omelette in the usual way and garnish with boiled vegetables, each in a separate little mound arround the dish: asparagus, little brussels sprouts, peas, etc. Pour a little melted butter over the vegetables. This makes a very elegant dish.

TORTILLA RELLENA A LA ROMANA

Stuffed Omelette Roman Style

4 Servings

9 eggs
4 oz. spinach purée (tinned
  or frozen spinach can
  be used)
2 oz. butter

4 anchovy fillets
1 oz. grated cheese
salt and pepper
1 oz. Parmesan cheese for
  garnish

This is an original dish, one omelette inside another. Leave
the anchovies for several hours in milk to de-salt. Beat up
3 eggs, season and mix with the spinach and chopped anchovies.

In another bowl beat up 6 eggs, together with the grated
cheese, season with salt and pepper. First make the small
omelette with 3 eggs and spinach. Do not make this one too
hard. Then make the second, larger omelette. Place the small
one inside the plain, large one and roll. Sprinkle with grated
cheese and serve hot.

Soufflé is, as we know, a French word, and the verb souffler means 'to blow up, to inflate, to whisper'. It has become a household word for a certain type of dish, the basis of which is the white of egg beaten up together with béchamel and varying in taste according to the ingredients used, such as cheese, fish, vegetable, etc. Soufflés have become an integral part of Spanish fare.

The success of the soufflé depends upon the beating up of the egg whites to the right firmness, on timing and on the right temperature of the oven. A soufflé must be eaten immediately, as it other-wise sinks, for as its name tells us, it is inflated and only a whisper.

A soufflé is always served in the dish in which it is made. The individual soufflé dishes are very attractive and can be bought in all the stores. Once the béchamel or foundation for the soufflé is ready, beat the white to a firm snow and mix. Pour the mass into a dish greased with butter and bake immediately in a hot oven. A large soufflé needs to bake for about twenty minutes and the individual soufflés ten to fifteen minutes (according to size and ingredients).

SOUFFLE DE PESCADO

Fish Soufflé

6 Servings

Any boiled fish can be used, cod, turbot, salmon, hake etc.

1 lb. fish	6 eggs
4 oz. butter	salt and pepper
1 tablespoon flour	½ pint milk

Make a béchamel with half the butter, the flour and the milk, simmer to thicken and add the boiled fish, flaked with a fork. Mix well and continue to simmer for 1 minute. Take off the fire and add the rest of the butter, which has been beaten up with the yolks. Beat the whites to a stiff snow and add. Pour immediately into greased soufflé dish and bake in hot oven. Serve as soon as ready (about 20 minutes).

Ham soufflé and Spinach soufflé are made in the same way as above.

SOUFFLE AL QUESO

Cheese Soufflé

4 Servings

6 egg whites
1 pint milk
4 oz. freshly grated
    Gruyère cheese

2 oz. flour
4 oz. butter
salt and pepper
dash of cayenne or nutmeg

Prepare a béchamel with 4 oz. butter, the flour and milk, remove from the heat, add the grated cheese, mix well and season. Beat up 3 yolks and beat over the heat till the béchamel is smooth and frothy. Beat up the egg whites to snow and add to the cheese béchamel, beating all the time. Immediately pour into buttered dish and place at the bottom of hot oven. When it has risen and turned golden, serve immediately (about 15 minutes).

SOUFFLE DE PATATAS

Potato Soufflé

8 Servings

3—4 large potatoes
8 oz. butter
¼ pint cream
4 oz. lean smoked ham

4 egg yolks
6 egg whites
salt and pepper
2 tablespoons melted butter

Boil the potatoes in their skins. Peel and mash well while hot in a deep dish, season, add the butter over a low fire, beating well. Add the cream little by little and season. Remove from the heat and add the finely chopped ham and the yolks. Beat well. Exactly 20 minutes before required, add the whites of egg beaten to stiff snow, pour into buttered dish and bake in the usual way. Serve immediately.

CANALONES, PASTA, PANCAKES, PASTRY

Canalones are made of the same paste as spaghetti, macaroni, etc., and though it is the Italians who are best known for their 'pasta', canalones are a typically Spanish dish. Many Spanish housewives make the pasta or dough at home, although the canalones can be purchased ready for filling in the Italian delicatessen shops.

The canalones are about 4 inches in diameter and after boiling they are filled with the most varied stuffings, and served up with sauces in many different ways.

TO MAKE CANALONES AT HOME

2 lb. flour   salt
4 eggs   a little water

This quantity will make about 12 servings, but it is more economical to make plenty as the canalones can be kept for later use.

Put flour and salt on to pastry board, make a well in the centre into which you pour the beaten-up eggs, add a teaspoon of lukewarm water and knead till all the liquid is absorbed; add another teaspoon of lukewarm water if the dough is too firm. Knead well for a few minutes and roll into a ball on to a well-floured board. Cut the ball into several slices, flour the rolling pin and carefully roll into very fine paste. When one piece is almost as thin as paper, hang a clean cloth or serviette over the back of a chair, flour to prevent sticking and hang the 'sheets' of paste over it, flouring each slightly. When the sheets of paste are dry, cut them into 4-inch squares and wrap in a floured cloth till ready to use. Home-made canalones take less time to cook than the ready-made types (about 5 minutes is enough).

CANALONES A LA ROSSINI

Canalones Rossini

6 Servings

canalones	1 calf's brain
4 chicken livers	stock
4 rashers streaky bacon	nutmeg
any available left-overs:	grated cheese
veal, pork or chicken	butter
1 onion	salt and pepper

First place the canalones in a large saucepan of salted boiling water. If the home-made kind are used, 5 to 7 minutes' boiling will be sufficient. If the packaged kind is used, 20 minutes will be required. Drain carefully to avoid breaking and lay open on the slightly floured kitchen table.

To make the stuffing fry the bacon, then in the bacon fat fry the chicken livers, chop these up fine with the meat and chopped onion, cut up the brain and fry till well mixed. Add a little stock or tomato sauce. Season with salt, pepper and a little nutmeg. Pass the whole through the mincing machine. Place a strip of the filling along the middle of the canalones and roll up. Place in a well-greased baking dish. Sprinkle with grated cheese and butter and place in a hot oven for a short while or under the grill.

CANALONES CON ESPINACA

Canalones with Spinach

4 Servings

canalones
1 lb. spinach purée (or
  1 large packet frozen
  spinach)

2 anchovies
1 egg yolk
½ cup thick béchamel
  sauce (see page 186)

Pound the anchovies in a mortar (a teaspoonful of anchovy paste can be used instead). Beat up the egg yolk, mix with the anchovy and the béchamel sauce and into this beat the spinach purée so that the mass thickens. Season and allow to cool before filling the canalones in the usual way. When filled and placed in a buttered baking dish, pour a little béchamel over the canalones. Bake in a hot oven for a short while. Serve as an entrée.

CANALONES CON JAMÓN

Ham Canalones

4 Servings

canalones	1 egg
8 oz. chopped ham	2 teaspoons tomato purée
1 onion	1 teaspoon chopped parsley
1 teaspoon flour	butter
1 dash nutmeg	salt and pepper
	Parmesan cheese

Fry the chopped onion and the chopped ham in a little fat, sprinkle with the flour, add the tomato purée and simmer, stirring to make the mass smooth. Beat up the egg together with the chopped parsley and add. Season with salt and pepper and a dash of nutmeg. Simmer for a few moments till the mass is firm. Allow to cool before filling the boiled canalones. Roll up, sprinkle with butter and grated Parmesan and heat through in a hot oven.

CANALONES CON PESCADO

Canalones with Fish Fillings

4 Servings

canalones
8 oz. of any white fish such as cod,
   turbot, etc. or any left-overs
2 hard-boiled eggs

4 oz. mushrooms or
   mushroom stalks
2 tablespoons milk
butter
salt and pepper

Flake the boiled fish with a fork, chop up the hard-boiled egg and the mushrooms very fine. Bind all this with 2 tablespoons milk and a little creamed butter, season and allow to cool before filling the canalones. Roll up, sprinkle with butter and place in a hot oven or under the grill for a short time.

This fish filling can also be made with a béchamel or if preferred tomato sauce; in short, with a little imagination delicious fillings can be made of any left-overs.

MACARRÓNES A LA ESPAÑOLA

Macaroni Spanish Style

4 Servings

8 oz. macaroni	1 small tin tomato purée
4 oz. margarine or lard	2 oz. Parmesan or
4 oz. ham	Gruyère cheese
1 onion	2 oz. breadcrumbs

When the water in a large casserole is boiling, put the macaroni in and boil for 20 minutes. In the meanwhile melt the lard or margarine, fry the chopped onion and the diced ham, add the tomato purée, diluted with a little stock or water, salt and pepper. Simmer. Drain the macaroni. Butter the top, put into a baking dish, pour the sauce over and mix well. Sprinkle with grated cheese and breadcrumbs and put under the grill till brown. Serve immediately.

FRITADA DE MACARRÓNES A LA CAPUCHINA

Macaroni Capuchina

4 Servings

8 oz. macaroni	cucumbers
1 garlic clove	capers
anchovies	salt and pepper
olives	2 oz. breadcrumbs
	oil

Cook the macaroni in boiling salted water for 12 minutes. Fry the garlic in oil, when golden remove and add some anchovies, chopped olives, chopped cucumbers and capers. Season with salt and pepper. Add the macaroni, which has been well drained, shake up well together and pour into a baking dish. Sprinkle well with breadcrumbs and oil. Put into hot oven till golden and serve hot.

PANCEQUE CON GAMBAS

Pancakes With Shrimps

4 Servings

3 tablespoons flour	salt
½ pint milk and water	butter or lard for frying
1 large egg	shrimps
	béchamel sauce (see page 186)

Sift the flour into a basin with the salt. Make a well in the centre, stir in enough milk and water with a wooden spoon to make a smooth batter. Beat well. Break in the egg and mix thoroughly, add the remainder of the milk and water and leave to stand at least an hour before cooking, or longer if possible. To fry, melt sufficient fat to cover the bottom of the pan. Pour in just sufficient batter to cover the bottom of the pan. The thinner the pancake the better. Cook on one side for about 2 minutes, when done remove from the stove and turn, either tossing or with a palette knife. When cooked on both sides, put in a dish in a warm place to keep hot till the other pancakes are ready. Have some shrimps in a little béchamel sauce ready, fill and serve very hot.

PANCEQUE A LA FRANCESA

French Pancakes

As above, filled with finely chopped mushrooms cooked in butter. Sprinkle with lemon juice and roll. Serve with fresh cream poured over each pancake.

PANCEQUE ITALIANA

Italian Pancakes

Make the pancakes very thin. Have some spinach purée ready, place some on each pancake, roll up and sprinkle with Parmesan cheese. Serve very hot.

PASTELITOS DE POLLO CON HOJALDRE FRITA

Fried Chicken Patties

4 Servings

Pastry

1 lb. flour	cold water
7 oz. fat or margarine	salt

Sift the flour into a basin with a pinch of salt. Make a well in the centre and rub in 5 oz. fat, add sufficient cold water to make a smooth batter, which is not too firm. Leave for 5 minutes before adding one more oz. fat, roll out, sprinkle lightly with flour and add another oz. fat. Roll out to required thickness and cut into squares.

Filling

½ boiled chicken	1 tablespoon raisins
3½ oz. margarine or fat	1 hard-boiled egg
1 onion	1 teaspoon granulated sugar
1 tomato	salt and pepper
8 olives	oil for frying

Cut the chicken into small pieces. Fry the onion till golden, add the chicken and the chopped, peeled tomato, simmer for a few moments and add the sugar, salt and pepper, chopped olives and seedless raisins. Cut up the hard-boiled egg and fold in. Put 1 tablespoon of this filling into the centre of the little pastry squares.

Place another square over as a lid, moistening at the edge to stick. Heat the oil in a deep pan or casserole (not to boiling point) simmer over a low heat till the pastry rises, then turn up the heat and fry till golden on both sides. Drain well and serve hot.

FRITOS DE CAMARONES

Prawn Pancakes

4 Servings

4 oz. flour
1 egg
1 teaspoon baking powder
pinch of salt

$\frac{1}{2}$ pint milk
8 oz. prawns
$\frac{1}{2}$ cup béchamel sauce
 (see p. 186)
grated cheese

Make some very thin pancakes by beating up an egg with the flour, milk, baking powder and salt. Allow the batter to stand for at least an hour before using.

In the meanwhile shell and cut up the prawns (or lobster) and bind with a thick béchamel. Spread some of this mixture on each pancake and roll up.

Arrange side by side in a dish and sprinkle with grated cheese. Keep warm in the oven or under the grill till all the pancakes are ready.

Pescado

A great deal of fish is eaten in Spain, and the fish markets in the ports and fishing villages are a delight to the eye. The silvery turbot, the mussels, lobsters, prawns, ink-fish and sardines gleam in their baskets like a painter's palette.

A Spanish housewife will set forth, with her maid carrying a basket, to choose fresh food for the day to make sure that only the best appears on her table. Fish ranks high on the list, for many Spanish dishes include fish, meat and fowl with rice.

The following tasty recipes will help to bring fish back to our own tables, for it has somehow been neglected lately, either as a first dish at a dinner party or main dish for the family dinner.

Freshness in fish is, of course, the very first essential and it is the seemingly simple things that are so vitally important in cooking fish. One of these is boiling. The most succulent fish can be rendered tasteless by wrong handling, while there is nothing more delicious than a really fresh piece of boiled turbot or hake with a slice of lemon, served with Hollandaise or Tartare sauce. There are several ways of boiling fish — here are two of them:

1. Take a large pan, as the fish should be well covered; bring the water to boil, add the juice of lemon and put in a slice of lemon and salt. Slip the fish in gradually so that the water continues to boil. Take care not to over-cook.

2. To boil salmon, mackerel, trout, cod or bass take a quarter pint of vinegar to two pints of water, salt and a sliced onion, a sliced carrot and a bay leaf.

CAZUELITAS DE LANGOSTINOS SAN RAFAEL

Casserole of Clams San Rafael

1 lb. shrimps	2 glasses white wine
12 clams	1 glass cognac
4 oz. rice	1 tablespoon tomato purée
10 oz. butter	6 shallots or 1 onion
1 cup grated Parmesan	1 garlic clove
cheese	¼ pint cream
2 tablespoons flour	salt and pepper
a bouquet of herbs	a dash of cayenne

This is rice with clams in individual baking dishes with Aurora sauce and garnished with shrimps, powdered with grated cheese and baked in the oven *au gratin*.

In a casserole put 4 oz. butter, fry the chopped garlic and chopped shallots or onion till golden, add the shrimps and then the cognac. Light this and when the flame dies down, add the wine and ½ pint water, the herbs, salt and pepper; cover and simmer for 10 minutes, then take out the shrimps, shell and put on one side.

To make the sauce, first grind the shrimp shells in a mortar, replace in the liquid, adding the tomato purée. After first mixing the flour with 4 oz. butter and the cream to a smooth paste, add and boil for 10 minutes, stirring all the while with a wooden spoon. Take the pan from the fire and strain the liquid through a sieve. The sauce should be thick, and if it is not sufficiently thick, continue to simmer, stirring all the time. Add a dash of cayenne.

In the meanwhile, boil the rice in the usual manner for 20 minutes, drain. Wash the clams well and boil for 5 minutes. When they have opened, take out of shells. Put the rest of the butter into a pan, heat and fry the rice together with the clams for a few minutes.

Then put two clams with rice into each dish, garnish with shrimps, pour the sauce over, sprinkle with grated cheese and bake in a hot oven till brown.

FILETES DE RODABALLO A LA ANDALUZA

Fillets of Turbot Andalusian Style

6 Servings

6 fillets of turbot	4 oz. butter
1 piece of fish (for stock)	2 tablespoons breadcrumbs
2 onions	1 garlic clove
8 oz. tomatoes	chopped parsley
4 oz. mushrooms	salt and pepper
2 sweet peppers	1 glass white wine

Flatten the fillets of turbot with a wooden spoon, place in baking dish, spread with butter and keep in cool place till ready to use. Boil piece of fish (or fish head for economy) with one onion and salt in sufficient water to cover. While boiling add white wine. To make good stock simmer for about 20 minutes. In the meanwhile chop the onion and garlic clove, clean and chop the sweet peppers; peel and cut the mushrooms; wash and cut the tomatoes into small pieces. Fry the onion till golden, then add the peppers and mushrooms; when these are tender add the tomatoes. Pour the stock, of which there should be about two tumblers full, over the turbot and over this the fried vegetables. Bake in a fairly hot oven for 25 minutes. The fish will be tender and the stock absorbed, but the dish will not be dry. To enhance the taste, a little lemon juice should be added before serving.

ZARZUELA DE PESCADO

Fish Stew

6 Servings

4 thick slices turbot or hake	6 tomatoes
12 shrimps or prawns or some slices of lobster	1 garlic clove
	parsley
12 mussels	1 lemon
2 onions	½ cup dry white wine
	oil for frying

Cut the turbot or hake into fairly small pieces. Shell the shrimps or prawns and the mussels. Fry the chopped onion with a little chopped garlic in oil till golden. Add the mussels and chopped tomatoes. When these are fairly tender add the rest of the fish together with the wine. While this is simmering add the juice of a lemon, salt and pepper. Serve immediately with boiled potatoes or rice.

FILETES DE LENGUADO FRITOS
A LA MARQUESA

Fried Fillets of Fish Marquesa

4 Servings

4 fresh Dover Sole or plaice
fat for frying
lemon juice

1 egg
1 teaspoon chopped parsley
flour or breadcrumbs

Cut off the heads of the sole or plaice, season with lemon juice, chopped parsley, salt and pepper before dipping into batter made with an egg beaten up with either flour or breadcrumbs. Fry in deep hot oil (when fat is used, add a teaspoon of oil). Serve immediately, garnished with slices of lemon and crisp fried potatoes.

RODABALLO MIRAMAR

Grilled Turbot Miramar

4 Servings

4 nice thick slices turbot
1 lemon
olive oil

mayonnaise sauce
  (see page 184)
flour
chopped parsley

Season the turbot with lemon juice, salt and pepper. Dust with flour and grill gently. Keep sprinkling with oil and lemon juice while grilling so that the fish does not get dry. Decorate with parsley and slice of lemon. Serve with mayonnaise sauce.

CALAMARES A LA BILBAINA

Bilbao Calamares Squids (ink fish)

4 Servings

24 small squids	1 tablespoon olive oil
2 onions	1 clove garlic
2 tomatoes	$\frac{1}{2}$ cup breadcrumbs
salt and pepper	1 teaspoon chopped parsley

Clean the squids in several waters, separate the ink-bags carefully and place the liquid in a cup.

Heat the oil in a saucepan and slightly fry the chopped onion, chopped garlic, tomatoes (previously peeled) and chopped parsley. Put the squids in this, adding sufficient water to cover; simmer till tender. In the meanwhile stir the ink with the breadcrumbs, salt and pepper, adding a little of the stock from the saucepan. When the squids are cooked add the ink, stir well while slowly bringing to the boil. Serve with slices of fried bread and boiled rice.

AILLOLI

Salt Cod with Mayonnaise

4 Servings

1 lb. salt cod	olive oil
3 cloves garlic	1 lb. boiled potatoes
1 lemon	8 oz. boiled carrots and peas
mayonnaise sauce	8 oz. boiled green beans
(see page 184)	

Soak the salt cod in water (overnight if possible). Cut in slices and place in cold water. Boil and then remove from water. Place in a dish with hot boiled vegetables over it. Then add hot or cold mayonnaise. Add salt and lemon juice.

RAPE A LA MONISTROL

Rock Cod Monistrol

4 Servings

2 lb. rock cod	1 tablespoon flour
½ pint milk	2 tablespoons olive oil
1 clove garlic	1 coffeespoon saffron
1 onion	salt and pepper

Chop the onion and the garlic up very fine and pound in a mortar with the saffron and a pinch of salt, then mix well with the flour and milk till smooth. Pour this over the fish and simmer till tender. Turbot or hake can be used instead of cod for this dish.

CROQUETAS DE PESCADO

Fish Croquettes

4 Servings

1 lb. boiled hake, turbot
   or cod (or any left-over
   boiled white fish)
1 onion
1 egg yolk

breadcrumbs
oil or fat
salt and pepper
1 teaspoon chopped parsley
$\frac{1}{2}$ cup béchamel sauce
   (see page 186)

Boil the fish in the usual way; it is tastier if $\frac{1}{2}$ glass white wine is added. Chop the boiled fish up finely with onion, parsley, salt and pepper. Add $\frac{1}{2}$ cup béchamel sauce and fold into the fish over a very low fire to thicken. The consistency should be firm but not dry. Roll into croquettes, allow these to cool before dipping into the yolk of egg and breadcrumbs. Fry in hot, deep fat till golden.

LENGUADOS AL PLATO

Sole in Casserole

3 Servings

3 fresh plaice
2 onions
4 oz. mushrooms or
   mushroom stalks
salt and pepper

1 glass white wine
1 cup stock
breadcrumbs
6 oz. butter

Grease a baking dish with butter, make a bed of finely chopped onion and mushrooms. Onto this lay the plaice, which has been washed and dried. Pour the white wine and the stock (or water) over the fish, cover with the rest of the onion and mushrooms and sprinkle lightly with breadcrumbs. Finally melt the remaining butter and pour over. Bake in a medium oven till tender (this should take about 15 minutes). Serve immediately with boiled potatoes.

MERLUZA AL HORNO

Baked Hake

6 Servings

6 slices hake
5 tablespoons concentrated tomato juice (purée)
½ cup white wine
1 tablespoon chopped parsley
¼ cup breadcrumbs

olive oil
salt and pepper
1 lemon

Prepare a thick tomato sauce with purée and white wine, season with a dash of salt. Grease a baking dish with oil. Lay the slices of fish side by side, pour the hot sauce over the hake and powder with breadcrumbs into which parsley has been finely chopped. A few drops of oil over this will prevent it from drying. About 15 minutes in the oven will suffice. Serve immediately in the same dish, with wedges of lemon.

MERLUZA A LA CATALANA

Catalan Hake

4 Servings

4 thick fillets hake
4 pieces fried bread
anchovy butter
1 cup tomato sauce

1 dessertspoon chopped parsley
oil for frying

Clean and dry the fillets of fish. Fry four pieces of bread in oil, the same size as the fillets. Grill the fillets and place each one on a piece of fried bread which you have spread with anchovy butter. Serve on individual plates with tomato sauce. Sprinkle with parsley. Any white fish can be used for this recipe.

PULPETAS DE LENGUADO

Stuffed Sole

4 Servings

2 large Dover soles
½ pint shrimps, prawns or
    a piece of lobster
1 egg
breadcrumbs

oil or fat for frying
¼ pint milk ⎫
2 oz. butter ⎬ for béchamel
2 oz. flour ⎭ sauce

This is an elegant dish for special occasions.

Wash the soles, which your fishmonger has filleted. Cut the fillets in half, so you have 8 long strips of fish. For the filling, first make the béchamel sauce in the usual way; this should be firm enough not to run. Into the béchamel beat the finely chopped peeled shrimps or prawns, season to taste and fill the fillets. Roll these up and tie with white thread or string. Beat up the egg and first dip the fillet rolls in egg, then into breadcrumbs and fry in deep fat or oil till golden. Snip off the thread and serve with tomato or Tartare sauce.

BACALAO A LA MAÎTRE D'HOTEL

Cod Maître d'Hotel

4 to 5 Servings

2 lb. dried cod
4 oz. butter
½ teaspoon chopped parsley
1 onion finely chopped
1 tablespoon flour

1 pint fish stock
1 lemon
1 lb. boiled new potatoes
dash of nutmeg
salt and pepper

Soak the cod for about 24 hours in cold water, changing the water several times. Place the cod in cold water and slowly bring to boil; take off the fire and leave in covered saucepan for about 10 minutes. In the meanwhile heat the butter in a frying pan, taking care it does not brown; slowly add the flour, stirring all the time with a wooden spoon so that it does not get lumpy. When smooth add the hot fish stock and onion, season with salt, pepper and nutmeg.

Take the cod out of the water and dry, take off the skin and place in the white sauce, which should only simmer, not boil, over a very slow fire for a few minutes. Garnish with parsley and slices of lemon. Serve with boiled new potatoes.

Fresh cod can also be used for this recipe. In this case place in boiling water and boil for 5 minutes till tender.

BACALAO A LA VIZCAINA

Dried Cod from Vizaya

4 Servings

2 lb. dried cod	8 tomatoes or 1 tin tomatoes
1 cup olive oil	3 garlic cloves
2 onions	2 pimentos or 1 tin
1 bouquet herbs	pimentos morrones
salt and pepper	$\frac{1}{2}$ pint stock

Cut the cod in pieces and soak overnight in cold water. Peel and take out the bones. Fry the chopped onions and garlic. Add the cod, the peeled tomatoes, the pimentos and herbs; when simmering, add the stock and simmer and then add sufficient water to cover. Cook slowly over a low fire for about $1\frac{1}{2}$ hours.

No Spanish cookery book would be complete without this tasty national dish from the North of Spain.

PESCADILLAS CECILIA

Small Hake Cecilia

4 Servings

4 small hake or 4 fillets of hake	salt and pepper
juice of 2 lemons	1 tin asparagus tips
flour	1 hard-boiled egg
olive oil	½ pint white sauce

This dish can be made with the whole fish or it can be filleted if it is made of pieces of large hake. Sprinkle with lemon
juice, flavour and baste in flour, fry in olive oil and garnish
with chopped boiled egg. Serve in a flat dish with asparagus
tips and white sauce.

MEJILLÓNES

Mussels

4 Servings

3 pints mussels	a bouquet of herbs (bay leaf, thyme and parsley)
½ pint water	1 chopped onion
½ pint white wine	1 tablespoon flour

Clean the mussels thoroughly and put them into a pan. Cover
with white wine and water, adding the chopped onion and
bouquet of herbs. Simmer till the shells are open; when they
have opened the mussels are cooked. Take the mussels out
and reduce the liquid if less is required. Remove half a shell
from each mussel. Bind the remaining liquid with the flour.
Flavour, adding a little more wine if necessary. Pour this
sauce over the mussels immediately before serving.

CAMARONES FRITOS

Fried Prawns

4 Servings

1 lb. large prawns	3 tablespoons breadcrumbs
1 egg	oil for frying
3 tablespoons flour	

After cleaning carefully and taking out of shell, turn the prawns in flour and then in beaten-up egg and breadcrumbs. Heat the oil and fry the prawns to a golden brown. Serve with boiled potatoes and mayonnaise.

ENSALADA DE LANGOSTA

Lobster Salad

4 Servings

1 small lobster (or piece left-over)	$\frac{1}{2}$ tablespoon capers
3 hard-boiled eggs	2 stalks celery
4 chopped olives	mayonnaise (see page 184)

Cut the lobster into small pieces, add chopped hard-boiled eggs, olives, chopped celery and capers. Pour in mayonnaise, mix gently with a wooden spoon and serve chilled.

ENSALADA DE CANGREJO

Crab with Lettuce

4 Servings

6 oz. crab meat
2 hard-boiled eggs
1 head lettuce
½ pint mayonnaise
  (see p. 184)
¼ pint chili sauce

½ breakfast cup chopped
  celery
1 tablespoon minced
  chives
dash of Worcester sauce
1 garlic clove

Mix the chili sauce, the chives and celery with mayonnaise, add a dash of Worcester sauce. Break the lettuce into shreds and toss into garlic-rubbed bowl. Top with flaked crab meat and sliced hard-boiled egg. Pour the sauce over and chill till served.

TRUCHAS RELLENAS A LA JIRONESA

Stuffed Trout in the Style of Jiron

4 Servings

Clean and cut open 4 trout, season with salt and lemon juice, stuff with the following stuffings: chopped olives, onions, tinned pimentos, almonds, peeled mushrooms, salt and pepper and a little oil and vinegar. Tie the fish up with thread, dip into oil or butter and breadcrumbs. Encase each fish in brown or greaseproof paper, which has been slightly greased on the inside. Tie again and place in the oven or under a slow grill, taking care the paper does not burn. Serve in the paper.

BUDÍN DE MERLUZA CON MAYONESA

Hake Pudding with Mayonnaise

8 Servings

2 lb. hake	4 eggs
1 lb. tomatoes or 1 large tin	parsley
4 onions	salt and pepper
4 oz. butter	1 lemon
¼ stale white loaf (6 slices)	1 garlic clove
1 glass milk	3 teaspoons oil

Boil 2 sliced onions, parsley, salt and pepper in 1 pint of water with lemon juice for a little while before putting in the hake. Simmer the fish slowly in a covered saucepan.

In the meanwhile soak the bread in hot milk. Fry 2 onions (chopped) in oil till golden, add the garlic clove and tomatoes, stirring till it thickens. Pass through a sieve and season.

Take the fish out of the stock, skin and take out the bones, flake with a fork and beat up with melted butter and the bread, which has been squeezed out, then add the tomato sauce. Beat up the egg yolks and add. Finally beat up the whites to fairly stiff snow and add. Pour the whole into a buttered ovenproof dish, which fits into a saucepan. Boil this in bain-marie. This pudding is also good baked in the oven.

Serve with a hot mayonnaise sauce if the pudding is served hot, or cold sauce if the pudding is served cold. Both are equally nice. The pudding can be garnished with shrimps or prawns.

This pudding can be made with any white fish.

LENGUADO A LA CREMA

Cream Sole

4 Servings

4 fillets Dover sole	2 eggs
grated cheese	2 tablespoons flour
½ pint milk	salt and pepper
	lemon juice

Place the fillets in boiling water with salt and lemon juice. Take care to keep the fillets whole. Place on heated serving dish, sprinkle with grated cheese.

In the meanwhile make a custard cream. Beat up the white of the eggs till stiff, then beat the yolks into the milk and carefully add the flour, simmer for a moment to heat and fold in the whites. Season to taste and pour over the boiled fillets. Serve immediately. This is a delicious dish.

PASTEL DE PESCADO ECONÓMICO

Fish Cake

Any left-overs of boiled fish can be used. Take out the bones and skin. Place in a casserole with white bread, which has been soaked in milk and squeezed. Add the yolks of 2 eggs, beat well and add chopped onion, parsley, salt and pepper. Place in a greased baking dish and bake (it can also be cooked in a double saucepan (bain-marie). Serve with tomato or caper sauce.

CORVINA A LA VASCA

Basque Eel

4 Servings

1 lb. eel	4 tablespoons vinegar
1 garlic clove	¼ pint oil
1 bay leaf	salt and pepper

Wash and cut the eel into pieces. Grill for a few moments, then fry in oil, adding the crushed garlic and bay leaf. Fry till brown, take off the fire and add the vinegar. Continue to simmer till the eel is tender. Serve in its own sauce, with boiled potatoes.

LENGUADO AL VINO TINTO

Sole in Red Wine

4 Servings

4 filleted soles	4 oz. mushrooms
4 oz. shrimps	2 glasses red wine
2 onions or shallots	1 lemon
	salt and pepper

Slightly fry the sliced onions and mushrooms. Place the fillets of fish in a large, flat baking dish, garnish with the onions and mushrooms, add the wine, salt and pepper, and cook slowly under a medium grill or in the oven till the fish is tender. Garnish with hot shelled shrimps and slices of lemon.

CORONA DE TOMATE CON MAYONESA
DE PESCADO

Tomato Ring with Fish Mayonnaise

6 Servings

2 lb. white fish (cod, hake or turbot)
2 cups mayonnaise (see page 184)
1 teaspoon fine herbs
3 tins tomato juice

1 tin tomato purée
2 leaves gelatine
1 teaspoon sugar
salt and pepper
1 lemon

Boil fish in salted water with the lemon juice till tender. Leave to get cold. When cool take the skin off and remove the bones, flake with a fork and mix with the mayonnaise and fine herbs. Dissolve the gelatine in hot tomato juice. Add the contents of the remaining two tins of juice into which the tomato purée has been stirred; season with sugar, salt and pepper. Pour into a ring mould and leave in the refrigerator, preferably all night. Turn out onto a large serving platter and heap the fish mayonnaise in the centre.

SALMON A LA ALICANTINA

Alicante Salmon

4 Servings

4 thick slices fresh salmon	2 sliced red peppers
1 lemon	parsley
olive oil	salt and pepper
	1 onion

Wash and dry the salmon and soak for 2 to 3 hours in a sauce made of ¼ pint olive oil, the lemon juice, sliced onion, salt and pepper, red peppers and a sprig of parsley. 20 minutes before serving take the salmon out of this pickling sauce, dry and grill till tender. Serve garnished with slices of lemon and Hollandaise sauce (see page 186). This should be served separately.

VERDEL REBOZADO

Mackerel

4 Servings

4 mackerel	breadcrumbs
1 egg	oil or fat for frying

Wash and cut open, so the fish lies flat. Dip into egg and breadcrumbs, deep fry in hot oil. Drain well and serve with boiled potatoes.

BACALAO A LA NAVARRA

Cod in the style of Navarra.

6 Servings

2 lb. dried cod	3 red or green pimentos*
¼ pint olive oil	2 garlic cloves
6 onions	3 red peppers
6 tomatoes*	

* (or a large tin pimentos morrones and 2 tins tomatoes)

Soak the cod in cold water for 24 hours, changing the water two to three times. Dice the onions and the pimentos together with the red peppers. Heat the oil in a large pan and fry the onions till golden, add the pimentos and peppers. Put the tomatoes in boiling water for a few minutes to make peeling easier. Peel and cut in quarters, add to the fried onions and pimentos and finally add the chopped garlic cloves. The vegetables should not be fried till they dissolve as this is not a sauce. Keep warm till ready to use.

    Cut the cod into strips and bring slowly to the boil, taking care that the pieces remain whole. Take the fish out of the water and place in a flat baking pan in which it can be served. Throw half the stock away and add the rest to the fried vegetables, mix this well and pour over the fish; leave in hot oven for about 10 minuts. Serve immediately.

SARDINAS FRITAS

Fresh Fried Sardines (or Sprats)

4 Servings

24 fresh sardines or 32 sprats   1 lemon
flour   parsley
oil or fat for frying

Clean and take the heads off. Dry well and salt. Dip into flour and deep fry. Drain well and serve with slices of lemon and garnished with parsley.

ARENQUES EN CAZUELA AL GRATIN DE TOMATE

Herrings in Casserole au gratin with Tomato

6 Servings

12 herrings   1 glass white wine
1 tablespoon oil   breadcrumbs
2 lb. tomatoes or 2 tins   salt
1 onion   1 clove garlic
   1 teaspoon parsley

First make the tomato sauce. Fry the chopped onion and garlic. Add parsley and the peeled or tinned tomatoes, the wine and the salt. Simmer. The sauce should be fairly thick. Then clean the herrings, take the heads off and dry. Pour some of the sauce in the casserole, into that put a layer of fish, more sauce, more fish. The sauce should cover the fish well. Sprinkle with breadcrumbs and a few drops of oil. Bake till done (about 20 minutes). Serve in the casserole.

Carne

Meat is generally the main course and consequently very important. In Spain it is seldom served as a simple roast or grill, and though it is true that a poor piece of meat can be made more palatable through clever cooking and garnishing, it can never be excellent unless the actual quality of the meat is good. In other words — you cannot make a silk purse out of a sow's ear. Also, however ornate the dish with sauces and garnishing, the ground work, that is to say the actual cooking of the meat, is all-important.

A few things to remember: to roast a large piece of meat the oven should be hot before it is put in to seal the juices in and once the meat is brown all over, the oven can be turned down somewhat so that it can cook right through.

For a small piece of meat the oven

should be very hot so that the meat is done quickly and does not have time to dry.

To boil, never put the meat in hot water; always start with cold and take off the scum when it comes to the boil.

The following meat recipes will convert our beef, veal, pork and lamb into succulent Spanish dishes.

CHULETAS DE TERNERA A LA ZINGARA

Veal Cutlets Zingara

6 Servings

6 veal cutlets	6 slices boiled ham
butter	2 cups Spanish sauce
2 cups stock	(see page 189)
salt and pepper	olive oil

Fry the cutlets in butter and 1 tablespoon of olive oil. This mixture prevents the meat from sticking to the pan. When brown on both sides, strain and add stock and the Spanish sauce, simmer for 30 minutes. In the meanwhile fry the ham in the butter and oil, take the cutlets out of the sauce, roll in the slices of ham. Place on serving dish, pour the sauce over and serve immediately.

TERNERA RELLENA

Stuffed Veal

8 Servings

3 lb. breast of veal	1 egg
2 lb. minced pork	1 cup centre of bread
8 oz. minced smoked ham	¼ pint milk
1 tablespoon chopped parsley	½ pint sherry or white wine
1 garlic clove	salt and pepper
1 onion	olive oil or butter

Soak the bread in milk and squeeze, then beat up together with egg and chopped parsley, salt and pepper. Put into a large bowl and mix with wine or sherry; fold in the minced pork and ham. The best way to mix this filling is with your hands.

Lay the breast of veal flat on the table. Spread the filling evenly, taking care not to fill too near the edges. Roll tightly and tie in the centre and at both ends with white string or thread.

Into a large casserole put the oil or butter and slightly fry a chopped onion and garlic clove. Put the meat roll into the hot fat and slightly brown on each side, then add the stock and white wine and slowly simmer for 2 hours. Watch to make sure there is sufficient liquid, otherwise add more stock, wine and some butter.

Snip the string off and serve in its sauce.

FILETES DE TERNERA

Veal Cutlets

Remove all gristle and fat from the cutlets. Veal should never be grilled, but fried or roasted. Heat a little butter, adding a drop of olive oil to prevent burning. Fry the cutlets till brown on both sides. Do not turn with a fork, but with a spatula or knife. Simmer till very well done and serve with vegetables and potatoes.

TERNERA EN CAZUELA CON BERENJENAS

Veal Casserole with Egg Plant (Aubergines)

4 Servings

2 lb. veal	2 oz. ham or bacon
1 onion	4 aubergines (egg plant)
2 tomatoes	olive oil
dash of cinnamon	herbs (thyme, bay leaf, marjoram)
1 tin little peas	1 glass white wine
(*petits pois*)	salt and pepper

Fry chopped veal in oil, with chopped ham or bacon, add chopped onion and the herbs. When well done add the tomatoes, cinnamon, salt and pepper and the white wine. Simmer and if necessary add a little water. Add the *petits pois* when almost ready to serve. In the meanwhile wash and slice the aubergines, dip in flour and fry. Serve separately as the veal is served in the casserole in which it is cooked. Of course, other vegetables can replace the aubergines if they are out of season. This dish is nice served with boiled rice.

GUISADO DE TERNERA

Veal Ragoût

4 Servings

1 lb. lean veal	1 onion
lard or margarine	4 oz. mushrooms
4 rashers bacon	$\frac{1}{2}$ pint stock
bunch of herbs	$\frac{1}{4}$ pint white wine
	nutmeg

Cut the veal into little squares. Fry the bacon, the onion and the herbs, add some fat and cook the meat slightly to close the pores. Add the wine, the mushrooms, the stock and a little grated nutmeg and simmer with the lid on till the meat is tender (about 1 hour). Serve with new potatoes and *petits pois*.

PIERNA DE CARNERO CON GUISANTES A LA ESPAÑOLA

Leg of Lamb with Peas Spanish Style

Rub the leg of lamb over with garlic, oil and rosemary. Put into the roasting pan with a little oil, salt and pepper and roast, first in a hot oven, then somewhat lower. Make a sauce with the liquid in the pan, mixed with a little tomato sauce, chopped smoked ham and tender *petits pois*. Serve very hot with roast potatoes.

REDONDO DE TERNERA AL HORNO

Roast Round of Veal

4 Servings

2 lb. best veal	1 small tin tomato purée or
4 oz. lard	4 tomatoes
2 onions	1 glass white wine
2 carrots	parsley
bay leaf	salt and pepper
2 rashers bacon	

Wrap the bacon rashers arround the veal, place in a roasting tin, add the sliced onion, carrot and the lard, and roast in a moderately hot oven. When half done, add the wine, bay leaf, sliced tomatoes or purée. Cover the roasting tin and return to a moderate oven, cook for 2 hours. When done put the sauce through a sieve. Season and re-heat. Carve and place on a serving dish, garnish with fried potatoes and parsley and serve the sauce separately.

TOURNEDOS CON DELICIAS DE QUESO

Tournedos Steaks with Cheese Balls

6 Servings

6 tournedos steaks
6 slices white bread
½ cup sherry sauce
   (see page 187)

3 eggs
3½ oz. grated cheese
breadcrumbs
olive oil
salt and pepper

Rub the steaks with oil and grill in the usual way, place each on a slice of fried bread (this should be well drained and not greasy). For the cheese balls: beat the white of eggs to snow, add the grated cheese, salt and pepper. Roll into little balls, which are first dipped into the beaten egg yolks and then into breadcrumbs. Deep fry. Make a little heap of these golden balls in the centre of the platter with the tournedos steaks all around. Pour a little sherry sauce over the meat and serve immediately.

TERNERA ENCEBOLLADA

Veal With Onions

4 Servings

2 lb. veal
3 oz. margarine or lard
1 garlic clove
2 onions

1 glass white wine
3 cloves
salt and pepper

Melt the fat in a saucepan. Brown the veal a little on all sides; add the whole onions, cloves, garlic and the wine. Cover and cook on a slow fire till tender. When done, take the garlic, cloves and onions out of the sauce, which should be thick and tasty. Serve with boiled potatoes.

ESCALOPAS DE TERNERA RELLENAS

Stuffed Veal Cutlets

4 Servings

4 large veal cutlets
1 egg
breadcrumbs

4 large slices cheese
oil or fat for frying

With a very sharp knife slice the veal cutlets open, leaving one end uncut. Choose a cheese that melts (like American cheese). Open the cutlet and slip a piece of cheese inside. Baste in egg and breadcrumbs and deep fry till golden. This dish, so simple to make, is very tasty. Serve with fried potatoes and vegetables.

LOMO DE CERDO RELLENO

Stuffed Pork Cutlets

As above, only use lean pork instead of veal.

HIGADO A LA FAVORITA

Braised Liver

4 Servings

1 lb. liver	1 clove garlic
1 onion	chopped parsley
1 carrot	lemon
8 oz. tomatoes	oil for frying
pepper	fried bread
sage and cloves	1 tablespoon breadcrumbs

Scald the liver in boiling water, drain and cut in slices. Heat the oil and fry the breadcrumbs and sliced onion and carrot until a light brown. Then add the liver, piercing a clove into each slice. Simmer and add a little sage, the tomatoes, garlic, salt and pepper. Almost cover with cold water and bring to boil, then put down the fire, cover the pan and simmer till the liver is tender. In the meanwhile fry four slices of bread till crisp. When the liver is ready, take out the cloves and the garlic and serve, garnished with the fried bread, slices of lemon and parsley.

BISTECS A LA ANDALUZA

Andalusian Beefsteaks

4 Servings

4 lean steaks for grilling	olive oil
2 aubergines	2 onions
4 oz. ham	4 large tomatoes
3 tomatoes or 1 small tin	½ cup rice
purée	butter

Rub the steaks with olive oil on both sides. Grill and season. Garnish with baked aubergines stuffed with ham, large tomatoes stuffed with rice and a sauce made with fried onions and tomatoes and the gravy from the steaks mixed with a little butter.

TOURNEDOS A LA CREMA

Creamed Tournedos

6 Servings

6 beef tournedos	¼ pint milk
4 tablespoons oil	1 egg yolk
1 onion	1 teaspoon chopped parsley
1 tablespoon flour	juice of 1 lemon
salt and pepper	butter

Fry the tournedos in oil, season and keep warm while preparing the sauce. Fry the finely chopped onion in butter, add the flour and the milk, stir till thick and add the beaten up yolk, the parsley and the lemon juice, season and pour over the tournedos. Serve with boiled potatoes.

CHULETAS DE CERDO A LA MADRILEÑA

Madrid Pork Chops

4 Servings

4 pork chops	1 bay leaf
4 tablespoons olive oil	marjoram
parsley	1 red pepper
2 garlic cloves	salt and pepper

Chop up the garlic and parsley, add the oil, bay leaf, marjoram, sliced red pepper and salt and pepper. Put the chops in this and cover the dish. Turn the chops from time to time so the herbs can penetrate both sides. Bake till done, basting so the chops do not get dry. Serve with fried potatoes.

CHULETAS DE TOCINO CON SALSA DE TOMATE

Pork Chops With Tomato Sauce

4 Servings

4 pork chops or cutlets	1 clove garlic
2 oz. flour	1 small tin tomato purée
3 oz. oil or fat	salt and pepper

Remove most of the fat from the meat and pound gently with the back of a wooden spoon or knife. Season with salt and pepper, dip both sides in flour, rub with garlic clove. Heat the oil in frying pan and brown the meat until it is tender. Keep hot while making the sauce. Dilute the contents of a small tin of tomato purée in $\frac{1}{4}$ pint boiling water (this can have a dash of sherry or white wine in it to improve the taste). Drain half the fat off, mix the rest with tomato purée and serve separately. This dish is good with boiled rice.

LOMO DE CERDO ENVUELTO EN COL

Ribs of Pork in Cabbage

4 Servings

1 white cabbage	1 onion
1 lb. pork ribs	8 oz. tomatoes
fat for frying	a little flour

Fry the meat till almost done, take off the bone. In the meanwhile put the cabbage to boil in salt water until almost tender, but taking care that the leaves remain whole. Drain and wrap the pieces of meat in a cabbage leaf, tying with cotton. Sprinkle with flour and fry. Serve with fried tomatoes and onion.

CHULETAS DE CORDERO A LA BECHAMEL

Béchamel Lamb Chops

4 Servings

8 lean lamb chops	olive oil
béchamel sauce (see p. 186)	breadcrumbs

Grill the chops till almost done, drain off the fat and wrap in béchamel sauce. Allow to cool slightly till firm enogh to dip in breadcrumbs. Fry quickly in hot oil till golden. Drain well and serve immediately.

This recipe can also be used for veal cutlets, only for veal fry instead of grilling.

COSTILLAS DE CERDO A LA PORTUGUESA

Portuguese Pork Chops

7 Servings

7 pork chops	olive oil for frying
1 onion	1 glass white wine
2 tomatoes	2 garlic cloves
bouquet of herbs	salt and pepper
1 small white cabbage	7 potatoes

Fry the chops over a medium fire, drain and keep hot. In a separate pan fry the chopped garlic and sliced onion. When golden add the peeled tomatoes, the herbs and the wine, salt and pepper, simmer until well done. Shred the cabbage and boil. Boil the potatoes. Serve the chops in a large dish garnished with the cabbage at one end and the potatoes at the other. Pour the vegetable sauce over the chops.

CHULETAS DE CORDERO VILAREAL

Lamb Chops Vilareal

5 Servings

10 lamb chops	1 lb. parboiled sliced potatoes
4 rashers of bacon	2 tablespoons stock
2 onions	salt and pepper
bouquet of herbs	oil for frying

Wash chops and flatten well with the back of a wooden spoon; fry over quick fire till brown on both sides. In another saucepan fry the rashers of bacon; when brown fry the sliced onions in the bacon fat with a sprig of herbs. Pour this together with the chops into a casserole, place the lid on firmly and bake in a medium oven. When almost ready, add the sliced, parboiled potatoes. When these are tender, serve very hot. If necessary a little stock can be added to this hot-pot.

CHULETAS DE CORDERO BRASEADAS A LA PAYESANA

Lamb Cutlets, Payesana

As above, using lamb cutlets instead of chops. When adding he sliced potatoes, also add boiled carrots and turnips. Serve very hot.

FIDEOS A LA CAZUELA

Chops and Spaghetti in Casserole

8 Servings

2 lb. thick, short spaghetti	2 onions
1 lb. Butifarra (garlic sausage)	2 tomatoes
2 lb. pork chops	2 oz. toasted hazel nuts
2 lb. pork sausages	1 red pepper
2 oz. fat or butter	2 Maggi cubes
2 oz. cheese	2 garlic cloves
½ coffeespoon saffron	1 teaspoon parsley
salt and pepper	2 tablespoons cocoa

In a large casserole melt the fat or butter, fry the chopped onion and garlic with the pork chops and the pork sausages; when brown add the sliced pepper (taking care to extract the seed), the chopped tomatoes, and the garlic sausage. Add a pint of water, salt and the chopped parsley. Dilute the saffron in a little of the liquid and add. Simmer for 20 minutes, then add the spaghetti. Dissolve the Maggi cubes in a little of the liquid and add. Pound the hazel nuts in a mortar, mix in the cocoa and add (this addition might seem strange, but it gives a delicious taste to the sauce and neutralises the fat). Boil till the spaghetti is tender and serve in the same casserole. Garnish with grated cheese.

ESTOFADO MONTAÑESA

Montañesa Stew

4 Servings

2 lb. stewing steak
2 oz. flour
2 onions
2 carrots
fat or olive oil

French mustard
2 tablespoons cocoa
bay leaf
salt and pepper

Cut the steak into 1-inch pieces, roll in the flour. Fry 2 onions
till golden, add the steak and fry till brown. Add sufficient
boiling water to almost cover, together with the sliced carrots
and bay leaf. Simmer for 30 minutes, add 1 teaspoon French
mustard to the sauce. Continue to simmer. When almost
ready to serve, take out half a cup of the liquid, mix the cocoa
and return to the stew, which should be rich and delicious.
Serve with boiled potatoes, spaghetti or boiled rice.

GUISO DE VACA CON COÑAC

Beef Stew with Brandy

6 Servings

2 lb. best fillet of beef
2 tablespoons butter
2 tablespoons brandy
4 oz. mushrooms

1 small tin tomato purée
¼ pint cream
salt and pepper
paprika

Melt the butter in a large casserole or stew-pan and brown the meat quickly on all sides. Pour in the brandy, set alight and shake the pan till the flame dies out. Pour in the stock, mixed with the tomato purée and chopped mushrooms. Stir, season and simmer for a few minutes, then add the cream, stir and put on the lid. Cook gently for 2 hours. Make sure from time to time that the stew is not dry, in which case add a little more stock.

LOMO DE CERDO A LA BATURRA

Fillets of Pork Baturra

4 Servings

2 fillets of pork
flour
oil or fat for frying
1 glass red wine

1 onion
4 oz. smoked ham
2 dozen olives
1 tablespoon tomato purée
2 hard-boiled eggs

Flour the fillets of pork and fry in hot oil till golden and well done all through. Drain well and keep hot. In the same oil fry the chopped onion and ham; mix the tomato purée with the wine and a little flour to thicken the sauce, add and stir while simmering. Add the meat again and at the last moment the chopped olives. These should not boil as they would get hard. Garnish with finely sliced hard-boiled egg.

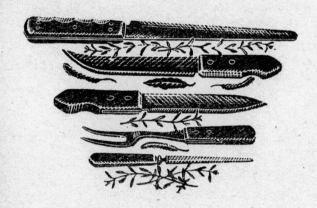

COCIDO A LA MADRILEÑA

Madrid Stew

4 Servings

1 lb. stewing steak
2 marrow bones
2 oz. bacon
6 oz. continental smoked
  boiling sausage
8 oz. chick peas

2 carrots
2 leeks
2 onions
2—3 potatoes
salt and pepper

Soak the chick peas overnight in plenty of cold water. Put the meat, marrow bones and bacon in cold water, salt and bring to boil. Take the scum from the top and add the peas. Boil for 30 minutes. Now add the finely cut vegetables and diced potatoes. Cover the pan and simmer over a low fire for at least 1½ hours. Cut the sausage into small pieces and put into the stew. Flavour to taste.

Pieces of chicken or any left-overs can be added to the cocido.

ESTOFADO DE VACA A LA CATALANA

Catalan Beef Stew

4 Servings

2 lb. stewing steak	1 small tin tomato purée
1 onion	3 glasses red wine
1 garlic clove	bouquet of herbs
salt and pepper	8 new potatoes
	garlic sausage or smoked ham

Fry the sliced onion and the garlic in lard or oil. When the onion is golden, throw the garlic away, put in the meat, cut into 1-inch squares, till well browned, then pour the whole into a deep casserole or saucepan with a lid, add the herbs, the wine and the tomato purée, diluted with a few tablespoons of boiling water and simmer for 30 minutes. Add more wine and continue to simmer, adding 8 new potatoes, a few pieces of garlic sausage or smoked ham and simmer till done. Serve hot in the same casserole.

MANITAS DE CORDERO A LA CATALANA

Calf's Trotters à la Catalana

4 Servings

4 trotters	1 egg
1 onion	breadcrumbs
1 garlic clove	oil or fat for frying
bouquet of herbs	salt

Boil the trotters in salt water, after washing thoroughly, for 15 minutes, throw the water away and put into fresh boiling water, salt, garlic clove and a bouquet of herbs. Simmer until tender. Drain, remove the bones and cut into pieces. Dip in egg and breadcrumbs, deep fry in oil or fat and serve with fried potatoes.

ROSCA DE CARNE

Meat Loaf

4 Servings

1 lb. minced beef	mixed herbs
4 rashers streaky bacon	1 onion
2 eggs	1 clove garlic
salt and pepper	breadcrumbs
	lard or dripping

Fry the chopped onion and garlic till golden. Throw away the garlic and mix the onion with meat. Beat up 1 egg and fold into the meat, with mixed herbs, salt and pepper. Roll the meat into a loaf and baste with the other egg and breadcrumbs. Place in baking pan, wrap the bacon over the roll and bake in a hot oven for 1 hour (add a tablespoon of fat to the pan). Serve with tomato sauce.

PICADO DE CARNE CON BORDEA DE PATATA

Chopped Meat with Potato Purée

4 Servings

Left-over beef or veal can be used for this dish. Cut the meat into little squares. Prepare a vegetable sauce with fried onion, pimentos, tomatoes, green beans, and any other vegetable in season. When this is well done, add the meat to heat.

Prepare the potato purée, by mashing up boiled potatoes very smoothly, add the beaten-up yolk of an egg and salt, simmer, adding a few drops of milk if required, beating well. The purée should be thick and creamy. Circle a large platter with the purée and put the meat and vegetable in the centre. It can also be served in a casserole, in which case sprinkle a little yolk of egg over the purée, and a few minutes in a hot oven will give it a lovely golden colour.

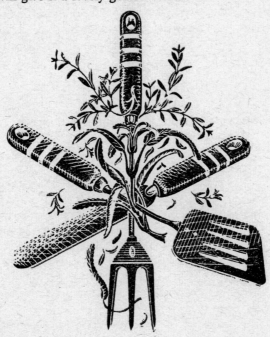

PAN DE CARNE A LA LIONESA

Lionesa Meat Loaf

4 Servings

1 lb. boiled beef or veal	fat
vegetables	2 eggs
1 tablespoon stock	2 tablespoons flour
	salt and pepper

This is a good dish to make when beef or veal are left over from the cocidos or soups.

Mince the meat, heat stock and stir in flour to a smooth paste; carefully stir in beaten-up eggs over a very low fire. Add the minced meat and mix well. Season to taste and put the mass into a greased pudding bowl or shape. Bake for 30 minutes, turn out of the shape and serve with tomato or other sauce.

CROQUETAS A LA ESPAÑOLA

Spanish Croquettes

4 Servings

8 oz. minced pork or ham
8 oz. minced veal or beef
¼ pint milk
1 tablespoon flour

1 egg
salt and pepper
oil for frying

It is important that the meat should be very finely minced -
this can be done when raw or cooked. Fry the meat in oil till
it is slightly brown. Drain and add the flour and milk, cook
till the liquid is absorbed and season to taste. Beat up the
egg and add to the paste. Heat till this too has been absorbed
in the paste. Mould into croquettes and roll these in breadcrumbs. Fry in deep fat or olive oil till golden and serve
with tomato sauce.

SALCHICHAS PANAMEÑAS

Panama Sausages

4 Servings

1 lb. minced pork
2 tablespoons grated onion
2 chopped garlic cloves
1 tablespoon chopped parsley
½ teaspoon red pepper

1 teaspoon cinnamon
3 cloves
¾ pint sweet wine
8 oz. brown sugar

Mix the finely minced pork with the grated onion, garlic and
the spices. Roll into little sausages. Boil the sugar in the
wine for 5 minutes, boil the little sausages in this syrup until
they turn black and the liquid thickens. Drain and serve hot.
These delicious little sausages can be served as an entrée with
rice or as a cocktail savoury.

PIMIENTOS RELLENOS CON CARNE
A LA BILBAINA

Stuffed Pimentos Bilbaina

6 Servings

6 large sweet pimentos
4 oz. minced pork
4 oz. minced veal
4 oz. smoked ham
2 slices white bread
1 egg yolk
2 onions

1 carrot
1 small tin tomato purée
1 glass white wine
salt and pepper
olive oil for frying
1 chopped garlic clove
flour

Prepare the pimentos by washing them and carefully cutting the top with the stem off. Extract all the seeds.

To prepare the sauce put some oil in a pan, fry 1 chopped onion and carrot and thicken with 2 tablespoons flour. Add the tin of tomato purée, diluted with the glass of wine. Keep warm till required.

To make the filling, fry 1 onion with the garlic clove till golden. Add the bread, which has been soaked in milk and squeezed dry, mix well till a smooth paste is formed, take off the fire and add 1 egg yolk, salt and pepper, and the meat. Fry till light brown and remove from the fire. Fill the pimentos and tie the tops on with thread. Put into flour and egg yolk and flour again. Deep fry in oil till tender. Drain and place in heated serving dish. Pour the sauce over and serve.

JAMÓN AL JEREZ CON ESPINACAS

Ham With Sherry and Spinach

As much boiled ham and spinach as required with sauce as follows:

2 carrots	4 oz. butter
2 onions	2 tablespoons flour
2 rashers bacon	2 tablespoons tomato purée
bouquet of herbs	½ pint stock
2 glasses sherry	salt and pepper

Chop up the onions and carrots and put into a casserole with the butter. Put in the herbs and simmer. Add the flour to thicken, then add the tomato purée and the stock. Simmer, take out the herbs and add the sherry. Pass through a sieve and put into a double saucepan to keep hot, for once the sherry has been added the sauce should not boil again. Make spinach purée in the usual way and serve together with bread croûtons.

LIEBRE EN ESCABECHE

Soused Hare

6 Servings

1 hare	3 chopped garlic cloves
olive oil	1 bouquet herbs
6 carrots	$\frac{1}{2}$ teaspoon peppercorns
2 onions	$\frac{1}{2}$ glass vinegar
1 glass dry white wine	2 tomatoes
1 lemon	salt

Cut the hare into pieces, salt and slightly brown in oil, place in a large casserole with the sliced carrots, onions, garlic, herbs, peppercorns, vinegar, wine and about $\frac{1}{4}$ pint oil. Cover the casserole and cook till the hare is tender. By then the sauce will be thick and greatly reduced. Prepared in this way the hare is just as delicious cold as it is hot. Serve with slices of lemon.

LENGUAS CON SALSA DE ALMENDRAS

Tongue with Almond Sauce

4 Servings

6 small lamb's tongues
1 onion
1 carrot
1 bay leaf
2 oz. butter or lard
juice of 1 lemon

2 large tablespoons flour
stock from the tongues
2 oz. chopped or ground almonds
1 oz. seedless raisins
salt and pepper

Clean the tongues well, boil in salt water with onion, bay leaf and carrot. When they are tender melt the fat in a casserole and stir in the flour, stir and simmer, add the stock from the tongues and bring to boil, stirring to avoid lumps. Add the ground almonds and the raisins and season with lemon juice, salt and pepper. Cut the tongues in half lengthwise, place them in a warm serving dish, pour the sauce over them and serve with boiled potatoes and vegetables.

FABADA

Pork and Beans

4 Servings

4 pork chops	olive oil for frying
2 large slices cooked ham	1 lb. haricot beans
4 slices Spanish sausage	4 slices black pudding
tomato sauce	1 garlic clove

Heat the olive oil in the pan with the garlic clove. When golden remove the garlic and quickly fry the chops until they are golden on both sides. Boil the haricot beans (previously soaked overnight) and put them into a deep casserole, moistened with a little tomato sauce (made from fresh tomatoes or purée). Add the chops, ham, black pudding and sausage. Cover and cook in a moderate oven for about 15 minutes.

POULTRY

Pollo

In a country where frozen food is still uncommon and where chicken farms turning out chickens by the thousand are as yet unknown, poultry is still considered a delicacy. Chickens in Spain tend to be small and scraggy, and Spanish poultry dishes treat it accordingly. Though chicken appears in many forms on Spanish menus it is frequently cooked in conjunction with meat, fish etc., as for instance in the Paella and other rice dishes.

However, just because it is a delicacy for them, the Spaniards very frequently serve chicken for their special guests — so if you go to Spain you will get plenty of chicken!

POLLO CON PISTO

Roast Chicken with Vegetables

6 Servings

1 tender chicken (about 4 lb.)	4 tomatoes
3 rashers streaky bacon	3 onions
3 oz. butter	2 pimentos (or tin of
salt and pepper	pimentos morrones)
a little fat or oil for frying	3 diced boiled potatoes

Place the chicken in a roasting pan. Fold bacon rashers on the breast and grease slightly. Put 1 teaspoon butter or oil in the bottom of the pan. Place in hot oven and roast for 1½ hours, basting from time to time.

Prick the breast with a fork; if no pink liquid comes out the chicken is done.

In the meanwhile, fry the onions in butter till golden, then the tomatoes and pimentos; finally add the diced potatoes. Serve this and any other vegetable in season with the chicken.

POLLO HERVIDO CON BECHAMEL

Boiled Chicken with Béchamel

6 Servings

1 boiling fowl	4 oz. butter
2 onions	2 oz. flour
1 lemon	$\frac{1}{2}$ pint milk
salt and pepper	4 oz. mushrooms
	nutmeg

Place the chicken in a large casserole or saucepan with just sufficient water to cover, salt and bring to boil, adding the chopped onions. When tender, taking care the chicken is not overdone, else it will fall apart, melt butter in a pan, stir in the flour gradually to a smooth paste and slowly beat in the milk. Add a little of the stock and the mushrooms, which have been fried in butter. Season with lemon juice and a dash of nutmeg.

Carve the chicken and place in a large serving dish in a ring of boiled rice, pour the sauce over the chicken and serve immediately. The stock can be served first as a clear soup, or a yolk of egg can be beaten up and added.

POLLO SALTEADO

Sauté Chicken

6 Servings

1 tender chicken	2 glasses white or red wine
1 small tin tomato purée	8 oz. butter
1 garlic clove	chopped parsley
new carrots	salt and pepper

Cut the chicken into eight or nine pieces, fry in butter till golden, season and add the crushed garlic clove, parsley and a few new carrots. Mix the tomato purée with the wine and add. Simmer for about 15 minutes, adding a little stock if necessary. Serve with new potatoes and little peas.

CONCHAS DE POLLO CON MAYONESA A LA ANDALUZA

Chicken in Shells with Mayonnaise, Andalusian Style

4 Servings

8 oz. cooked breast of chicken or left-overs	crisp lettuce leaves
4 tomatoes	1 cup mayonnaise
3 sour-sweet gherkins	parsley
3 hard-boiled eggs	4 shells or individual dishes
a few radishes	

Chop up the chicken, the gherkins, 2 eggs, parsley and 2 tomatoes. Mix with the mayonnaise. Line the shells with crips lettuce leaves, lay thin slices of tomato over the lettuce and pour in the mayonnaise mixture. Garnish with finely sliced egg, radishes and tomato.

PATO A LA ANDALUZA

Andalusian Duck

6 Servings

1 duck	butter
8 oz. chick peas	4 tomatoes
2 onions	1 pimento
1 garlic clove	1 tablespoon vinegar or
pinch black pepper	$\frac{1}{2}$ glass wine

Soak and boil the chick peas in the usual way. Separately boil the duck with a sliced onion in water. Carve when done. In the meanwhile crush 1 onion, garlic clove, tomatoes, pimento and a little black pepper in a mortar. Put some butter into a large casserole and fry the crushed onion etc., pour in the chick peas with half their water and 1 teaspoon vinegar or $\frac{1}{2}$ glass white wine, simmer and season to taste. Add the duck and simmer for 1 minute. Serve with vegetables prepared separately.

PATO CON ACEITUNAS

Duck with Olives

5 to 6 Servings

1 tender duckling (about 2½ lb.)	2 glasses white wine or Madeira
8 oz. butter	1 large tin tomato purée
2 oz. flour	4 dozen olives
4 onions	chopped parsley
6 carrots	salt and pepper
1 pint stock or water	oil

Duck is only nice when it is young and tender, otherwise it tends to be tough and insipid. Melt the butter with a spoonful of oil in a large casserole, put in the duck, well cleaned and washed, together with sliced onions and carrots. Cook till golden on all sides (about 20 minutes). Take care not to break the skin with a fork, so the duck does not lose its juice, and take care the butter does not burn. When golden, take the duck out and put aside. Slowly add the flour to the butter, stirring to smooth paste, add the wine and the tomato purée (the purée can be diluted with a tablespoon of hot water or stock) stir well and replace the duck in the casserole, add parsley and season, add the stock, using discretion not to make the sauce too liquid. Simmer for about 1 hour. When time to serve, add the stoned olives to the sauce. These should first be immersed in hot water for a few minutes so they are not cold, but they must not boil as they would get hard.

PATO ASADO A LA MALTESA

Maltese Roast Duck with Orange

5 to 6 Servings

1 tender duckling	1 glass wine
1 tablespoon butter	3 oranges
salt and pepper	1 teaspoon cornflour
	watercress

Clean the duck well, place in a baking dish with a little butter, salt and pepper. Roast in a hot oven for about 40 minutes, basting from time to time. When done put the duck on a heated platter and keep warm while preparing the sauce. To the juice in the baking dish add wine and the juice of 1 orange, stir well with the cornflour, simmer till the sauce is nice and thick. In the meanwhile slice the remaining 2 oranges. Put in boiling water for a minute to heat. Garnish the platter with orange and watercress or parsley. Serve the sauce separately. The duck can also be served already carved with the sauce poured over it.

PATO ALCAPARRADA

Duck With Caper Sauce

6 Servings

1 duck	$\frac{1}{3}$ cup capers
2 onions	$\frac{1}{2}$ cup blanched almonds
4 oz. butter	4 tomatoes
$\frac{1}{2}$ cup stoned olives and raisins	salt

Wash duck well and boil with an onion and salt. Carve into pieces and take off the bone. Melt the butter in a casserole, chop up an onion and fry with peeled tomatoes. When done add the pieces of duck and simmer. Add the almonds, capers, stoned olives and stoned raisins. Add sufficient hot stock from the duck to just cover. Simmer till much of the stock has evaporated and the remaining sauce is thick. Serve hot.

Legumbres

The basis for many Spanish dishes is the sanfayna, a sauce made from the vegetables of the land: onions, tomatoes, pimentos and courgettes fried in oil. This is used to garnish anything from meat and poultry to fish and rice. Otherwise vegetables are usually served on their own as dishes in their own right and consequently undergo more elaborate preparation than the average boiled vegetable served with meat.

When cooking vegetables it is important to avoid overcooking. Leave the vegetables firm; they look better and taste better.

To peel tomatoes, place them for a few seconds in very hot water and with the point of a knife remove the skin.

Do not chop up onion till just before using it. Use garlic with discretion; it is often sufficient to rub the bowl with it.

[141]

TARTA DE CEBOLLA

Onion Tart

8 oz. flour	6 large onions
1 teaspoon baking powder	2 eggs
pinch of salt	$\frac{1}{4}$ pint milk
3 oz. fat	3 rashers streaky bacon
lemon juice	

Make a short pastry with the flour sieved with baking powder, shortening fat, cold water and a few drops of lemon juice. Cut the bacon into pieces and fry. Finely mince the onions and stew in the bacon fat without browning, then cool and drain. Mix well with the eggs beaten up in the milk, and season. Line a baking dish with the pastry and pour in the onion filling. Bake in a hot oven for about 30 minutes, when the pastry will be done and the onion mixture golden brown.

TARTA DE LEGUMBRES

Mixed Vegetable Tart

pastry as above	chopped cooked leeks or onions
spinach purée	sliced cooked potatoes
margarine or butter	grated cheese

Line a baking dish with pastry as above and fill with a layer of spinach purée, then a layer of chopped cooked leeks or onions and finally a layer of sliced, cooked potatoes. Sprinkle with a little margarine or butter and a thin layer of grated cheese. Bake in a quick oven until the pastry is done and the top nicely browned. This is a delicious dish.

ESPARRAGOS SEVILLANOS

Asparagus Sevilla Style

Clean the asparagus and cut off the hard ends. Fry a garlic clove in oil together with a slice of bread. Take the garlic and the bread out of the oil and put in the asparagus with a little hot water. Simmer till tender. Season with salt. In the meanwhile crush the garlic and the bread up with a little vinegar. Add a chopped hard-boiled egg and serve with the asparagus.

ESPARRAGOS MIMOSA

Asparagus Mimosa

4 Servings

2 lb. asparagus	chopped parsley
3 hard-boiled eggs	2 cups salad dressing
	salt

Cook the asparagus in salted water till tender (tinned asparagus can also be used). Drain well and arrange on a serving dish. Cut the whites of egg into thin strips and sprinkle over the tips of the asparagus. Mince or mash the yolks and sprinkle over the whites. Keep cool till required. Mix chopped parsley with the French dressing and serve together.

ESPARRAGOS BELLA ELENA

Asparagus with Pancake Belle Helène

4 Servings

1 lb. or 1 tin asparagus
2 large or several small
pancakes (see p. 75)

1 cup thick béchamel
sauce (see p. 186)

Cut the asparagus into pieces about 1 inch long. Cut the
pancakes into strips, mix the two in a serving bowl and pour
the béchamel over. Serve hot.

COLIFLOR AL GRATIN

Cauliflower Au Gratin

4 Servings

1 large white cauliflower
4 oz. butter
1 tablespoon flour
½ pint milk

salt and pepper
nutmeg
½ cup grated cheese

Boil the cauliflower until fairly tender. Cut into several large
sprigs. Melt the butter and add the flour, stirring to smooth
paste, add the milk, continue to stir over low fire till it
thickens, season with salt, pepper and nutmeg. Put the
cauliflower pieces into a baking dish, pour the sauce over.
Sprinkle thickly with grated cheese and a little melted butter,
and bake in hot oven till brown.

BUDÍN DE COLIFLOR A LA BURGUESITA

Bourgeois Cauliflower Pudding

6 Servings

1 cauliflower	2 eggs
3 oz. butter	1 cup béchamel sauce
4 oz. ham	(see p. 186)
1 carrot	French mustard
1 truffle	parsley
	salt and pepper

Grease a ring-shaped pudding tin. Place pieces of truffle, ham and carrot alternately along the top. Boil the cauliflower, cut in small pieces and simmer in butter, adding the rest of the chopped ham and chopped parsley. Mix with béchamel sauce seasoned with a little French mustard. Add the egg yolks. Beat up the whites still stiff and fold in. Pour the mixture into the pudding form and bake for 20 minutes. Turn out and serve with other vegetables in the centre, such as mixed peas and carrots or baked tomatoes and mushrooms. It makes a very elegant vegetable dish.

COLIFLOR CON MAYONESA

Cauliflower with Mayonnaise

4 Servings

1 cauliflower	6 olives
2 hard-boiled eggs	mayonnaise

Boil and drain the cauliflower. Cool and place in a serving dish in small pieces. Garnish with chopped stoned olives, chopped hard-boiled eggs and cover with mayonnaise.

CACHITOS DE COLIFLOR

Cauliflower Pieces

4 Servings

1 large cauliflower	1 egg
1 cup béchamel sauce	breadcrumbs
(see p. 186)	oil or lard for frying

Boil the cauliflower in salt water till tender, drain, season and allow to cool. Cut into pieces or little bunches, allow to cool. In the meanwhile make the béchamel sauce. Dip each little bunch into the sauce and then into breadcrumbs. Beat up the egg. Dip the pieces of cauliflower in and again into breadcrumbs. Deep fry in oil or lard.

Serve with small boiled potatoes and pour the remaining sauce over the potatoes.

BERENJENAS SALTEADAS

Aubergines Sautés

6 Servings

½ cup oil	1 tablespoon stock
1 onion	salt and pepper
6 aubergines	2 tomatoes or 1 small tin

Fry the chopped onion; when golden add the aubergines sliced into large rounds, simmer for 5 minutes, then add the stock and the tomatoes. Season, cover and simmer very slowly until done.

BERENJENAS RELLENAS

Stuffed Egg Plant (Aubergines)

6 Servings

6 large aubergines	1 egg
oil for frying	chopped parsley
1 onion	breadcrumbs
garlic sausage	salt and pepper
1 slice white bread	milk

Cook aubergines in boiling salt water until tender, but not too much as they must remain firm. Cut in half and scoop a little out of the centre. Fry the chopped onion, then the garlic sausage (minced meat can be used instead) soak the bread in milk, squeeze and beat together with the egg, add to the meat and onion and the scooped out meat of the aubergines. Season well. Fill the aubergines which have been placed in a greased baking dish. Dust with breadcrumbs and a few drops of oil and bake for 5 minutes in a medium oven.

FRITOS DE PATATAS

Potato Fritters

4 Servings

2 lb. potatoes	salt and pepper
1 egg	oil or fat for frying
3 tablespoons flour	

Peel and wash potatoes, grate while raw and place in a colander to drain. Allow to stand for at least 1 hour, press the water out. Beat up egg and mix, add the flour to bind and season. Deep fry in fat or oil. Drop 1 tablespoon at a time into the oil, flatten with a wooden spoon to form little fritters. When they are crisp and golden, lay to drain on brown paper. Serve as savoury sprinkled with cheese or as a potato dish with the main course.

ALCACHOFAS DE JERUSALEM AL GRATIN

Jerusalem Artichokes Au Gratin

4 Servings

4 cups diced boiled Jerusalem artichokes	½ teacup melted butter mushroom sauce
1½ cups breadcrumbs	(béchamel with mushrooms added. See p. 186)

Butter a baking dish. Place the artichokes in it. Pour the sauce over the artichokes. Fry the breadcrumbs in butter till golden and sprinkle over. Place in a moderate oven for 3 minutes to heat.

ALCACHOFAS A LA CUSSY

Artichokes Stuffed and Fried

6 Servings

6 large artichokes	¼ pint milk
2 chicken livers	breadcrumbs
2 eggs	oil
1 tablespoon flour	nutmeg
1¼ oz. butter	salt and pepper
	lemon juice

Take the outer leaves off the artichokes, leaving the heart and a few of the tender leaves encircling it. Immediately submerge in lemon water to retain colour. Boil in the lemon water with salt. Make a béchamel sauce with 1 oz. butter and milk (see page 186). Season with salt, pepper and nutmeg and add the cut up chicken livers, simmer and add the yolk of 1 egg, simmer till sufficiently thick and season. Fill the artichokes with the mixture. Sprinkle the artichokes with flour, dip into egg and then into breadcrumbs. Deep fry in oil. Drain well and serve with slices of lemon.

ALCACHOFAS GUISADAS A LA ESPAÑOLA

Artichokes Cooked in the Spanish Style

6 to 8 Servings

8 artichokes
3 tablespoons oil
3 onions
¼ pint (scant) white wine
¼ pint (scant) vinegar

½ cup stock
½ tablespoon flour
bay leaf
salt and pepper
lemon juice
1 garlic clove

If the artichokes are big, take off all the leaves, and if they are small and tender only take off the outer leaves, and cut off the ends. Rinse well in water and lemon juice, drain and dry. Slightly fry finely chopped onions in the oil and put in the artichokes, but do not allow the onion to get brown. Add vinegar and wine and simmer till the liquid has evaporated, leaving only about 3 tablespoons. Add the stock, garlic clove and a bay leaf, cover and simmer till the artichokes are tender (about 30 minutes). Thicken the sauce with a little flour, stirring well to avoid lumps. Cook for another 2 minutes. Take out the bay leaf and the garlic and serve immediately.

ALCACHOFAS A LA SEVILLANA

Seville Artichokes

4 Servings

12 artichokes
8 oz. new potatoes
oil for frying
3 garlic cloves
½ teaspoon saffron

½ tablespoon flour
stock
1 lemon
dash of vinegar
salt

Peel the leaves off the artichokes leaving the hearts only; submerge in lemon juice and water to keep white. Fry the garlic in oil till golden; take out of oil. In the meanwhile peel the potatoes. Toast the saffron by putting it into a hot oven for a few minutes. Pound the garlic and the saffron in a mortar with salt, a few drops of water or stock and vinegar. Take the artichokes out of the lemon water and drain. Put them into the oil in which the garlic has been fried, together with the new potatoes, and simmer; add the flour mixed with 1 tablespoon stock and the garlic and saffron paste. Mix well and cover to simmer slowly till tender, but taking care that the artichokes and potatoes remain whole.

PUERROS AL GRATIN

Leeks au Gratin

6 Servings

2 lb. leeks	¾ pint milk
6 oz. butter	salt and pepper
1 tablespoon flour	nutmeg
1 tablespoon tomato purée	breadcrumbs

Cut the green stalk off the leeks, wash and boil for about 15 minutes till tender. Drain well. Put 4 oz. butter in a casserole and melt; add the flour, stirring with a wooden spoon. Gradually add the milk, stirring to avoid lumps. When it comes to the boil add the tomato purée and put in the leeks. Season with salt, pepper and the nutmeg. Simmer gently till the sauce is thick. Add the rest of the butter and sprinkle with breadcrumbs. Put into a hot oven for a few minutes to brown.

Celery can be cooked in the same way.

JUDIAS VERDES A LA CASTELLANA

Castilian Green Beans

green string beans	garlic
pimentos	parsley
olive oil	salt and pepper

Cook the green beans in boiling salt water till tender. Cut up and fry the pimentos in oil, together with a chopped garlic clove and chopped parsley. Drain the beans and mix with the fried pimentos.

JUDIAS VERDES A LA RIOJANA

Green Beans Riojana

4 Servings

2 lb. green beans	1 onion
4 pork chops	garlic
4 rashers streaky bacon	flour
8 slices garlic sausage	salt and pepper
	oil

Fry the bacon slightly (it should not be crisp), put in the chopped onion and garlic; when golden add the chops and fry till brown. Thicken the sauce with a little flour and add the sausage. In the meanwhile put the beans to cook in boiling water with salt; when tender drain off most of the water leaving about one-third. Add the chops, etc. from the frying pan and allow the whole to simmer for a few minutes till the water has been absorbed. Serve with boiled potatoes.

PANACHE DE ESPINACAS

Panache of Spinach

6 Servings

2 lb. spinach or 2 packets frozen spinach	oil for frying
3 hard-boiled eggs	6 slices white bread
	salt and pepper

Boil the spinach well, chop and pass through a sieve, season. Fry the slices of bread in oil till crips, put the spinach on the fried bread at the last moment so it does not get soggy. Chop up the hard-boiled eggs and garnish the spinach.

APIO AL BECHAMEL

Celery in Béchamel

6 Servings

8 oz. celery	½ tablespoon flour
2 oz. butter	¼ pint stock
salt and pepper	¼ pint milk
sugar	a dash of nutmeg

Take the celery leaves apart, cut off the green, wash and scrape well till white. Cut into squares. Melt half the butter; put the celery in to simmer; add the stock and a pinch of sugar, nutmeg, salt and pepper. Cover till it comes to the boil, then lower the heat and allow to simmer for 1 hour (or less if tender). In the meanwhile make a béchamel sauce with the rest of the butter, the flour and milk. Drain the celery, pour the sauce over and serve hot.

COLES DE BRUSELAS A LA MORNAY

Brussels Sprouts Mornay

4 Servings

2 lb. sprouts	½ pint Mornay sauce
1 oz. butter	(see p. 192)
	grated cheese

Wash the sprouts, removing stem and outer leaves. Cook in boiling salted water. Drain well and season. Pour a little melted butter over the sprouts and place in a baking dish. Pour Mornay sauce over, sprinkle with grated cheese and put in a hot oven for a few moments to brown.

CALABACINES AL HORNO

Baked Courgettes

6 to 7 Servings

6 courgettes	1 garlic clove
olive oil	breadcrumbs
	salt and pepper

Take 6 medium-sized courgettes: clean carefully and cut off stem end. Cut in half. Rub round a baking dish with the garlic clove, then place courgettes in a dish with 2 tablespoons oil. Season with salt and pepper and sprinkle a little oil over the top. Bake in a medium oven till tender. Baste with the oil, sprinkle with breadcrumbs and brown in oven. Serve hot.

COLES DE BRUSELAS A LA CREMA

Creamed Brussels Sprouts

2 Servings

2 lb. sprouts	2 tablespoons cream
2 oz. butter	salt and pepper
½ pint milk	

Clean and boil the sprouts for 10 minutes. Drain and put to boil gently in milk. Add the butter and the cream but do not boil again. Season and serve hot.

PATATAS FINAS

Boiled Potatoes with a Difference

2 lb. potatoes   1 lemon
1 hard-boiled egg   salt and pepper
1 oz. butter

Boil potatoes in the usual way; drain. Melt butter in a pan; remove from fire, add the lemon juice, salt and pepper. Stir in finely chopped hard-boiled egg. Toss potatoes in this mixture and serve very hot.

PATATAS AL GRATIN CON QUESO

Potatoes au Gratin with Cheese

6 Servings

2 lb. potatoes $\frac{1}{2}$ pint béchamel sauce
4 oz. ham.   (see p. 186)
2 oz. butter   1 oz. grated cheese

Place the boiled, diced potatoes in a buttered dish, in alternate layers with the chopped ham. Cover with béchamel sauce and sprinkle with grated cheese. Put into a hot oven to brown and serve.

BERZA RELLENA A LA CAMPESINA

Stuffed Cabbage Campesina

1 large white cabbage	2 garlic cloves
1 lb. minced pork or beef	2 tablespoons lard
8 oz. minced ham	salt and pepper
1 glass white wine	2 onions
1 pint stock	2 egg yolks
mixed herbs	

Wash the cabbage and boil for 5 minutes. Drain carefully
and separate into parts of five or six leaves each. In the
meanwhile mix the minced meat with the ham, 1 chopped
onion and garlic, bind with egg yolks and season. Wrap this
in the leaves and tie with thread. Melt lard in a large casserole
with 1 chopped onion and herbs. Cook the cabbage rolls till
brown, then add wine and stock. When it comes to the boil
turn the fire down and slowly simmer for 2 hours or more.
Pass the sauce through a sieve and serve with the cabbage.

CALABACINES EN POTAJE

Stewed Courgettes

8 courgettes	½ chopped onion
2 garlic cloves	salt and pepper

Peel the courgettes, slice and boil in salt water till tender.
Fry the chopped onion and garlic; when golden put in the
courgettes which have been drained. Season and serve.

CALABACINES RELLENOS A LA VEGETARIANA

Vegetarian Stuffed Marrow

6 Servings

3 medium-sized marrows · ½ cup milk
1 oz. flour · 1 tin asparagus tips
2½ oz. butter · 1 onion
1 egg yolk · 1 small glass sherry
nutmeg · breadcrumbs
salt and pepper

Peel and wash the marrows and halve lengthways; boil for 10 minutes. Scoop out some of the flesh to make little boats. Melt half the butter, add flour and milk and season; cook for 5 minutes. Beat in the egg yolk and add the asparagus. Fill the marrows and place in a greased baking dish. Sprinkle with chopped onion and breadcrumbs, pour the sherry in the dish with the rest of the butter. Bake gently for 30 minutes.

CALABACINES RELLENOS A LA ANDALUZA

Andalusian Stuffed Marrows

8 Servings

4 medium-sized marrows · breadcrumbs
2 onions · salt and pepper
4 oz. minced meat · 12 olives
2 hard-boiled eggs

Peel the marrow, cook and cut as above. In the meanwhile fry the onion, the meat and the scooped-out marrows; add the hard-boiled egg and breadcrumbs. Deep fry in oil, drain well and serve hot. A tomato sauce can be served with the marrow.

PATATAS RELLENAS A LA MARIETA

Stuffed Baked Potatoes Marieta

6 Servings

6 large potatoes
8 oz. minced meat or left-overs
2 oz. butter
1 onion
½ oz. flour

¼ pint broth
½ glass white wine
1 teaspoon vinegar
1 teaspoon chopped parsley
salt and pepper

Wash and bake the potatoes whole, turning them from time to time so that they do not burn. In the meanwhile fry the chopped onion in butter till golden and sprinkle with flour, add the broth and the wine with the vinegar and a little pepper. Keep this sauce warm till required. Cut the meat up fine with parsley if already cooked. If raw minced meat is being used fry with a little parsley until golden. When the potatoes are sufficiently baked carefully cut off the tops and take out most of the flesh. Mash up with a fork and add to the meat and sauce. Simmer for a few moments and fill the potato shells - it is always a good idea to bake a few more potatoes than required in case one or other of the shells break. Cover with the tops and bake in a medium oven for 15 minutes. Serve very hot.

CEBOLLAS RELLENAS

Stuffed Onions

4 Servings

4 large white onions 1 tablespoon lard
8 oz. minced pork   ¼ pint broth
3 egg yolks   salt and pepper
1 teaspoon chopped parsley

Peel and boil the onions in salt water for 5 minutes, drain and carefully cut out the centre leaving fairly thick. Shell, fill with the minced pork which has been beaten up in the egg yolks with parsley, pepper and salt. Place in a greased baking dish, pour the broth over and bake in a medium oven till tender, basting from time to time.

LECHUGAS AL JUGO

Lettuce in Gravy

5 Servings

3 lettuces or 5 tiny ones 5 rashers streaky bacon
4 oz. carrots   1 tablespoon butter
2 onions   ½ cup stock
bouquet of herbs   salt and pepper

Wash the lettuce well in between the leaves, leaving the lettuce whole if possible. Drain and press out the water. Put salt, pepper and herbs in between the leaves. Tie with cotton so they do not fall apart. Fry the bacon and the chopped onions and carrots in the bacon fat in a casserole. Put the lettuce in and cover with stock and a little butter. Simmer gently until the lettuce is tender. Untie the string and serve hot.

REPOLLO CON MANZANAS

Red Cabbage with Apple

1 small red cabbage	salt and pepper
3 cooking apples	$\frac{1}{4}$ pint vinegar
4 oz. butter or margarine	caraway seeds
1 tablespoon sugar	

Wash and shred the cabbage, take out the white stalk and boil for 1 hour in plenty of salted water. Add vinegar and the sliced apples. Simmer for another hour. Season with salt, pepper and sugar. When tender drain off the water (this makes good vegetable stock), add the margarine or butter, simmer for a few more minutes and add a tablespoon of caraway seeds. This cabbage is delicious with roast duck, venison or sausages. White cabbage can be cooked in the same way.

CROQUETAS DE PATATAS

Potato Croquettes

1 lb. potatoes	1 teaspoon chopped parsley
butter	breadcrumbs
milk	oil for frying
1 egg	salt and pepper
1 tablespoon grated cheese	

Wash and boil the potatoes. Cream well with a little butter and milk, add the chopped parsley and season. Roll into croquettes, sprinkle with grated cheese, baste in egg and breadcrumbs and deep fry in hot oil. Drain well before serving.

JUDIAS VERDES A LA LIONESA

Green Beans Lionesa

4 Servings

2 lb. green string beans   2 small onions
4 oz. smoked ham   chopped parsley
3 oz. butter   salt and pepper

String, cut and wash the beans well. Boil in salt water for 20 minutes, drain and dry. Chop up the onions and ham, fry gently in butter till golden. Add the beans, shaking in the pan so they do not stick. Sprinkle with chopped parsley, serve in a heated dish.

PASTEL DE TOMATE

Tomato Flan

6 Servings

2 lb. tomatoes or 1 large tin   1 garlic clove
2 onions   short pastry (see p. 77)
4 rashers streaky bacon   salt and pepper
1 egg   mixed herbs
parsley   sugar
2 courgettes or small marrows   grated cheese

Line a baking dish with short pastry and bake for 5 minutes. In the meanwhile fry the bacon and the chopped onions and garlic in the bacon fat. Remove the bacon when crisp. Add the peeled and sliced tomatoes, 1 tablespoon chopped parsley, the sliced courgettes, a pinch of mixed herbs salt and pepper and a pinch of sugar. Simmer until soft, add the chopped bacon, pour the mixture into the pastry. Beat up the egg and pour on top, sprinkle with grated cheese and bake in a hot oven till the pastry is done. Serve hot.

ROLLO DE SANFAYNA

Vegetable Roll

6 Servings

2½ lb. potatoes	½ pint mayonnaise
2 onions	4 oz. mushrooms
2 pimentos	oil or fat for frying
3 tomatoes	salt and pepper
8 oz. courgettes	

Peel and boil the potatoes till tender. In the meanwhile fry the chopped onions, tomatoes, courgettes, pimentos and mushrooms till tender. Season. Drain off all fat. Lay a serviette or clean teacloth on the table, cover one half with the potatoes. Fold the serviette and pass the rolling pin over it to mash the potatoes into a thin, flat strip. Open the serviette and spread the mixed fried vegetables over the potatoes, then carefully lift the serviette at one end to roll the potatoes over the vegetable mixture. Place this potato roll on a platter to get cold. Pour the mayonnaise over it and you will have a colourful and tasty dish. When serving cut in slices.

GUISANTES CON JAMÓN A LA ESPAÑOLA

Ham and Peas in the Spanish Style

8 Servings

2 lb. peas (*petits pois*)	1 carrot
2½ lb. ham	oil
1 onion	salt and pepper
1 lettuce	

Fry the finely chopped onion and the carrot till golden; add the chopped ham and the chopped lettuce and the peas. If tinned peas are used not much time is required for boiling. If frozen or fresh peas, cook for about 30 minutes. Simmer till all the vegetables are tender, and serve as a dish on its own with meat or eggs.

Arraz

It is naturally in the part of Spain where rice grows that the most interesting rice dishes are to be found and from whence they originate — along the coast between Alicante and Valencia. The famous Paella or Valencian rice is a dish which can range from the most luxurious meal garnished with chicken and every type of sea food, to the poor man's staple diet and a means of making use of scraps of food of every description. The Spaniards, better than anyone, have discovered that rice enhances the taste of the food and spices with which it is cooked, such as saffron and tomatoes. On the whole one must not seek in Spanish recipes for the secret of turning out first class food in a few minutes with no trouble, for Spaniards know that really good food is always some trouble and a labour of love — and so with this

[165]

in mind and a little imagination real miracles can be performed with rice as a basis. A rice dish is very personal, for no two people turn out an identical Paella.

The great characteristic of Paella, so called after the dish in which it is made, is the diversity of ingredients used, ranging from all kinds of fish, shell-fish, chicken, meat, chicken livers, to pimentos etc. It is considered one of the national dishes, though it originated in Valencia and it is also called Arroz a la Valenciana (Valencian Rice).

There are many variations of this succulent dish. On the following pages are two of them, adapted for our kitchen, because the original Paella is cooked over a charcoal fire. We give also a few other Spanish rice dishes.

PAELLA

Spanish Rice

6 Servings

1 pint mussels
1 pint prawns
1 small cooked lobster
a few chicken livers
12 black olives
a few pieces of cooked
  white fish
1 garlic clove

12 oz. rice
2 onions
4 tomatoes
2 red or green pimentos
olive oil
a few crawfish or tinned
  clams
saffron

Heat the oil in a Paella or large iron frying pan, fry the sliced onions till golden, add the chopped garlic, pimentos, stoned olives and chicken livers. Over this, which should be well liquid with oil, pour the rice, fry till the oil is absorbed, then add the lobster, clams, white fish, prawns, boiled mussels and tomatoes. Add ½ pint boiling water into which a little saffron has been dissolved. Simmer over a low fire till the rice is tender; this should be when all the liquid has evaporated. Serve immediately.

PAELLA VALENCIANA

Valencian Rice

6 Servings

1 tender chicken	8 oz. garlic sausage (chorizo)
1 dozen snails or clams	2 garlic cloves
1 dozen mussels	1 tablespoon saffron
1 tin artichoke hearts	2 large breakfast cups rice
1 tin small peas (*petits pois*)	4 large breakfast cups water
	olive oil
1 small tin tomato purée	1 small tin pimentos morrones (sweet peppers)

Cut the chicken into 6 or 8 pieces. Heat about $\frac{1}{2}$ pint best olive oil in a Paella or large iron frying pan. Add the chopped garlic and cook the chicken slowly, basting all the time till golden; then gradually add the rice and cook for 15 minutes. By this time the rice will have turned slightly golden. Add the 4 cups boiling water into which the saffron has been dissolved (incidentally the amount of water used is always double the amount of the rice). Add the tomato purée and then the snails or clams and the mussels. Cook for about 15 minutes and then add the artichokes and peas. Cook for 5 minutes and then garnish with strips of pimentos and garlic sausage. Cook for another few minutes till the rice is tender and the liquid has dissolved. The secret of the Paella is to serve immediately, before the rice gets too dry.

ARROZ A LA PAMPLONESA

Rice Pamplona Style

4 Servings

1 onion	8 oz. tomatoes or 1 small tin
2 dry red peppers	2 cups rice
8 oz. cod	4 cups boiling water
salt and pepper	sweet peppers
1 tablespoon saffron	olive oil

Fry in olive oil chopped onion, dry red peppers and a piece of cod; season with salt and pepper. When this is well done, add tomatoes or small tin of tomatoes and then the rice. Continue to fry till the rice is golden, add sliced sweet peppers, boiling water (double the amount of that of the rice) and saffron. Boil for 15 minutes and finish by placing for 5 minutes in a hot oven.

ARROZ A LA CRIOLLA

Argentinian Rice

4 Servings

2 cups Patna rice	1 onion
8 oz. minced meat	oil or lard for frying
3 tomatoes or 1 tin tomatoes	1 garlic clove
or tomato purée	

Slowly pour rice into 2 pints boiling water. Boil fiercely for 20 minutes. Drain the rice through a colander and rinse with boiling water. Place in a large dish with a well in the centre for the meat sauce. For this fry a chopped onion and garlic clove and tomatoes or tomato purée and minced meat. When the meat is brown and well done, add a tablespoon of water if the sauce is too thick.

ARROZ BLANCO

Boiled Rice

Put the rice in a colander under the cold tap to remove any
loose starch, which would make the grains stick together.
Drain well and gradually sprinkle into boiling salt water so
that the water does not stop boiling. Boil fast for 15—20 minutes, taking care not to overcook. The cooking time varies
according to the quality of the rice and the quantities used.
Allow roughly $1\frac{1}{2}$ oz. per person. Always boil in plenty of
water. When done, strain and pour boiling water through the
rice to separate the grains.

ARROZ ESTILO BARCELONÉS

Rice Barcelona Style

3 Servings

8 oz. margarine
1 onion
4 oz. ham
2 tomatoes or 1 small tin
nutmeg

1 large cup rice
4 oz. *petits pois* (or 1 small
  tin)
chopped parsley
salt and pepper

Melt the margarine in a large casserole and fry the chopped
onion till golden; add the ham and sliced tomatoes. Put in
the rice and fry till it changes colour then add $2\frac{1}{2}$ cups boiling
water or stock (always $2\frac{1}{2}$ times the amount of liquid to rice).
Boil rapidly for 7 minutes, when the liquid will be almost all
absorbed. Add the boiled or tinned peas, season and finish
cooking in a moderate oven for about 10 minutes.

ARROZ ABANDA DE VALENCIA

Valencia Rice with Fish

4 Servings

8 oz. fresh cod	1 clove garlic
8 oz. hake	$\frac{1}{2}$ teaspoon saffron
8 oz. shrimps or crawfish	salt and pepper
1 onion	oil for frying
2 cups Patna rice	

Boil all the fish together. In the meanwhile fry the chopped onion and garlic clove n a little oil, add the rice and fry till golden. Add the fish stock and saffron, and boil. Keep the fish warm till required. When the rice is tender serve, either together with the fish or put the fish in another dish and serve with piquante or tomato sauce.

ARROZ CON POLLO

Rice with Chicken

6 Servings

1 boiling fowl	2 cups béchamel sauce
2 large cups rice	(see p. 186)
1 onion	nutmeg
	salt and pepper

Boil the chicken till tender, but be careful not to overcook. Boil the rice in the usual way. Make a fairly liquid béchamel with the chicken broth, milk and 1 egg yolk. Line a large serving bowl with the rice, carve the chicken into reasonable pieces, place on top of the rice, pour over the béchamel and serve hot.

MOROS Y CRISTIANOS

Moors and Christians

(Black Beans and Rice)

4 Servings

8 oz. black beans	1 onion
8 oz. rice	4 oz. chorizo or other
oil for frying	garlic sausage

Soak the beans overnight. Boil in the same water for about 2 hours. In the meanwhile fry the onion in a little oil, add the rice, simmer for a few minutes add double the amount of boiling water. Boil for 20 minutes. Drain well and add to the beans, which should only have a little thick sauce left. Continue to boil together for a few minutes, adding slices of sausage.

ARROZ A LA PRIMAVERA

Vegetable Rice

4 Servings

8 oz. rice	1 small cauliflower
1 tin asparagus tips	8 oz. new carrots
8 oz. *petits pois*, or 1 tin artichoke hearts	2 cups Hollandaise sauce (see p. 186)

Boil the rice and each of the vegetables separately. The cauliflower should be cut up into little bunches. When all is ready, garnish the rice with separate mounds of vegetables. Serve with hot Hollandaise sauce. These vegetables can be varied, of course, according to the season.

ARROZ CON MENUDILLAS

Rice with Giblets

4 Servings

1 lb. rice	giblets or chicken livers
2 oz. ham	1 glass wine
1 small tin tomato purée	oil for frying
1 onion	sweet herbs
salt and pepper	grated cheese
butter	

Boil the rice in the usual way. In the meanwhile chop and
fry the onion, giblets and ham with salt and pepper and sweet
herbs. When done add the tomato purée diluted in a teaspoon
of butter and the wine. Simmer for a few minutes. Make a
circle of the boiled rice on the serving dish, put the giblets in
the centre and serve with grated cheese.

ARROZ FRITO

Fried Rice

1 cup rice	2 oz. margarine or
1 onion	olive oil

Fry the chopped onion till tender, but do not let it turn brown.
Add the rice and fry, shaking well so it does not catch. When
the rice has absorbed the fat add 2½ cups boiling water. Season
and simmer slowly for 20 minutes. The water will be absorbed
and the rice will be tender with each grain separate. Serve
with fish or chicken.

ARROZ A LA ITALIANA

Italian Rice

4 Servings

8 oz. rice	6 oz. butter
4 oz. sausages	2 onions
4 chicken livers	2 oz. grated cheese
2 tablespoons tomato purée	2 pints stock
	salt and pepper

Melt 3 oz. butter in a casserole. Fry 1 chopped onion till golden, add the rice and shake. Add the boiling stock, season and boil for 20 minutes. Just before it is ready add the cheese.

In the meanwhile fry the sausages with the other chopped onion and the chicken livers; add the tomato purée with a spoonful of stock and simmer slowly for 15 minutes. Serve on a large platter surrounded by the rice.

ARROZ CON ALMEJAS

Rice with Mussels (or Clams)

6 Servings

1 lb. rice	1 tablespoon chopped parsley
1 lb. mussels or clams	1 head or piece of cod
2 tablespoons oil	1 onion
2 garlic cloves	1 carrot
salt and pepper	1 teaspoon saffron

Boil the cod's head, the carrot and the onion in sufficient water to make the stock. Simmer for $1\frac{1}{2}$ hours.

Finely chop the parsley and the garlic cloves and fry together with the saffron. To open the mussels put in boiling water, take out of shells and add to the fried garlic and saffron. Add the fish stock and bring to boil, then turn heat down and simmer for a little while. Bring to boil again and add the rice, gradually, so it continues to boil. There should be double the amount of liquid to rice. Boil for 15 minutes, then put into a warm oven and leave there for about 10 minutes before serving to dry the rice completely.

HÍGADO CON ARROZ

Liver With Rice

4 Servings

1 lb. calves' liver	3 tablespoons flour
2 onions	a little sage
1 glass red wine	salt
5—6 tablespoons oil or fat	

Cut the liver into thick slices and turn in salted flour. Fry in the heated oil or fat with a little sage. When the liver is cooked, remove from the pan and cut into very small pieces. Fry the chopped onions till golden, thicken with flour and add the wine and about half a cup of water to make the sauce. Simmer for a few moments and return the liver to the sauce to heat. Serve hot with boiled rice.

Ensalada

Salads are often served as a separate course as well as an accompaniment to the main dish, and though salad is often defined as a dish of raw vegetables and lettuces, this is not necessarily the case. A salad need not be restricted to raw food, as the following recipes go to prove. As a matter of fact, a cookery book can only indicate and awaken the imagination and creative instinct of the cook — for there is no end to the number of combinations which go to make a good salad.

No ready-made dressings are ever bought by the Spanish housewife, who has an almost unlimited number of combinations, which can so easily be made and enhance the quality and make the taste and character of the salad. The basic ingredients are olive oil, vinegar, salt and a pinch of sugar.

[177]

ENSALADA VALENCIANA

Valencia Salad

Cover a large platter with crisp lettuce leaves. Make a mound of finely sliced, firm tomatoes in the centre. All around place alternately radishes and sliced cucumber. Garnish with sliced hard-boiled egg and slices of lemon. Season with salt and pepper and lemon juice.

ENSALADA DE ACHICORIA

Chicory Salad

Wash several crisp heads of chicory in lemon water and chop into small rounds. Rub a salad bowl with garlic, put the chicory in with some chopped green olives and a finely chopped pimento. Season with the following dressing:

½ clove garlic	2 tablespoons olive oil
salt and pepper	1 teaspoon chopped tarragon
sugar	or mint
1 lemon	1 teaspoon French mustard

Pound the garlic, add the mustard, salt, pepper and a pinch of sugar. Stir in gradually the lemon juice. Into this gradually blend in olive oil and chopped mint. Pour over the salad.

ENSALADA RUSA

Russian Salad

2 cooked beetroot	1 tablespoon capers
5 boiled potatoes	4 apples
6 sour sweet cucumbers	1 celery
1 lettuce	2 hard-boiled eggs

This makes a delicious salad for a cold buffet or cold dinner. Finely chop everything together and mix, leaving out the eggs and 1 beetroot. The dressing can be a French dressing or a light mayonnaise. When the salad is mixed, garnish on top by chopping the white of egg, the yolk apart and making a design on the top with this and chopped beetroot.

ENSALADA DE ARENQUE

Herring Salad

As above, adding chopped smoked herring or rollmops.

ENSALADA A LA BOHEMIA

Bohemian salad

1 lettuce	1 truffle
8 oz. boiled string beans	4 oz. ham
1 hard-boiled egg	1 cup mayonnaise sauce

Wash and shred the lettuce. Chop the beans, the ham and the truffle. Pour over the mayonnaise and garnish with finely sliced boiled egg.

ENSALADA DE REPOLLO

Cabbage Salad

1 white cabbage	½ cup cream
oil and vinegar	2 eggs
salt and pepper	parsley
1 garlic clove	

Wash a small white cabbage and cook in salted water. Drain well and shred finely. Rub a salad bowl with garlic and put in the cooled shredded cabbage.

Make a dressing with three parts olive oil, one part Tarragon vinegar, salt and pepper. Gradually add well-beaten eggs and cream. Simmer gently in a double saucepan (bain-marie). Pour the hot dressing over the cabbage and leave to cool. Sprinkle with finely chopped parsley.

ENSALADA DE VERDURAS EN SORPRESA

Surprise Vegetable Salad

1 lb. diced boiled potatoes	1 cup French dressing
1 tin *petits pois*	2 leaves gelatine
1 small white cauliflower	tomatoes
mayonnaise (see p. 184)	

Mix cold diced boiled potatoes and tin of *petits pois* with a cupful of mayonnaise. Melt gelatine leaves and add. Put this mixture into a circular mould and leave in the refrigerator for some hours to set. In the meanwhile boil the cauliflower, leave to get cold. Turn the vegetable mould out onto a large platter, place the cauliflower in the centre, season with French dressing, garnish all around with fine slices of tomato and serve chilled.

ENSALADA LIDIA

Lidia Salad

1 pear
2 apples
1 orange
1 tablespoon chopped nuts
1 lettuce
chopped parsley and chives

2 boiled potatoes
small bunch grapes
3 tablespoons milk
2 tablespoons vinegar
salt and pepper
French mustard

Peel and dice everything together, and season with dressing made as follows. Beat up milk with salt, pepper, mustard and vinegar. Add a pinch of sugar and a sprinkling of chopped parsley and chives. Serve chilled.

ENSALADA DE ESCAROLA A LA ALMORAIMA

Endive Salad Almoraima

endives
1 lemon
1 garlic clove
green and black olives
1 hard-boiled egg

red pepper
salt and sugar
3 tablespoons olive oil
1 tomato
2 tablespoons vinegar

Choose tender, white endives. Chop every leaf in two and immerse in water with lemon juice. Crush garlic clove, a red pepper, salt and a pinch of sugar with a couple of drops of olive oil into a smooth paste, add peeled tomato. Mix vinegar with olive oil and mix all this well together. Chop in some green and black olives. Drain the endives well, pour the sauce over and garnish with hard-boiled egg. Serve very cold.

ENSALADA RAQUEL MELLER

Raquel Meller Salad

1 cucumber
6—8 tomatoes
some fillets of smoked herrings
vinegar and oil
mustard

salt and pepper
sugar
chives
parsley

Peel the cucumber and cut in very fine slices. Salt and place in a flat dish with a heavy plate over the cucumber to press out the water. Leave cucumber like this for a few hours and then drain off the water. Alternate in a salad bowl with thin slices of firm tomato, garnish with fillet of smoked herring and season with salad dressing made of three spoonfuls of oil to two of vinegar, a pinch of mustard, salt and pepper and a pinch of sugar. Sprinkle with finely chopped or grated chives and parsley. Serve cold.

ENSALADA LIRIO DEL VALLE

Lily of the Valley Salad

Chop up celery, apples, tomatoes, nuts and if available, a chopped breast of chicken. Mix with a light mayonnaise.

ENSALADILLA DE TOMATES Y PIMENTOS VERDES A LA ANDALUZA

Tomato and Pimento Salad Andalusian Style

Boil the pimentos for 5 minutes, cool and cut in strips. Submerge the tomatoes in boiling water, peel and cut into fine slices. Arrange in a salad bowl and garnish with a vinaigrette sauce with plenty of grated onion, apple, parsley, a hard-boiled egg and cucumber.

Sauces

Good sauces require careful handling and often the use of herbs for delicate flavouring. In this case nothing can replace the mortar and pestle for crushing the garlic, the sweet marjoram and other herbs, which lend such a mysterious, delicious flavour to so many Spanish sauces.

The Spaniards make the daily meal an event, for it is not merely a matter of riches, but of the right attitude. Food is not just swallowed in silence — it is an occasion for a family reunion and exchange of ideas, and it is a relaxation. The glass of wine is never missing and even if the meal is not sumptuous, it is prepared with care and served with good sauces.

SAUCES

SALSA MAYONESA

Mayonnaise Sauce

2 eggs yolks	vinegar or lemon juice
salt and pepper	1 teaspoon mustard
$\frac{1}{3}$ pint olive oil	lemon

Put the egg yolks into a china bowl, stir in a pinch of salt and pepper. Add the oil to the eggs drop by drop and stir all the time with a wooden spoon. Quite soon the mixture starts to thicken, then the oil can be poured in a steady stream, stirring the whole time. Add 1 teaspoon mustard. This will prevent the sauce from curdling. Add a few drops of vinegar or lemon juice. Be careful not to use too much vinegar. Very important things to note are: be careful not to leave any white in the yolks. This will make the mayonnaise too thin. If you add the oil too fast it will separate from the egg. If this happens break a fresh yolk into a clean bowl! and gradually add your curdled mayonnaise. It is advisable to use the mayonnaise on the day it is made, and if there is some over, keep it in a cool place, but not in the refrigerator.

SALSA TARTARA

Tartare Sauce

6 Servings

2 egg yolks
½ pint olive oil
2 tablespoons vinegar
1 tablespoon finely chopped capers

1 tablespoon finely chopped gherkin
1 teaspoon chopped parsley
1 teaspoon estragon
3 teaspoons French mustard
salt, cayenne pepper

Make a mayonnaise in the usual way with the yolks, oil and vinegar, then mix in the finely chopped capers, gherkins, parsley, etc. If the sauce is too thick dilute with a few drops of water.

SALSA A LA BEARNESA

Sauce Béarnaise

6 Servings

4 tablespoons vinegar
4 tablespoons white wine
5 oz. butter
shallots or onions
1 clove garlic (optional)

3 egg yolks
parsley and estragon
salt and cayenne pepper
mixed herbs

Very finely chop the shallots or onions, garlic, parsley and mixed herbs, simmer in the vinegar and wine, season with salt and pepper, allow to cool and add the yolks, beating well with a whisk. Return to the fire, put in a double saucepan (bain-marie) and add the butter. Stir well. This is a tasty sauce of mayonnaise consistency. It should be served hot with fish or meat.

HOLANDESA

Hollandaise Sauce

6 Servings

4 egg yolks   1 tablespoon lemon juice
3 tablespoons cold water   salt and pepper
4 oz. butter

Beat the egg yolks well with the cold water. Put into double saucepan (bain-marie) to heat, beating all the while till frothy. Add the melted butter, continue to beat. Add the lemon juice, salt and pepper to taste and beat over the fire till sufficiently thick. This sauce is generally used for fish.

BECHAMEL

Béchamel Sauce

6 Servings

2 oz. butter   2 oz. flour
½ pint milk   salt and pepper
nutmeg

Melt the butter in a saucepan, taking care not to let it turn brown, blend the flour gradually, stirring with a wooden spoon to make a smooth paste; add warm milk little by little, stirring over a very low fire. Season and serve immediately it is sufficiently thick.

SALSA AL MADEIRA O JEREZ

Madeira or Sherry Sauce

6 Servings

7 oz. butter
2 tablespoons chopped shallots
1 teaspoon flour
½ pint stock

½ pint sherry or Madeira
parsley
1 Maggi cube
salt and pepper

Melt the butter in a little casserole together with the chopped
shallots, simmer and add the flour, stirring to make a smooth
paste. Now gradually add the wine, simmer for 5 minutes,
add the hot stock and a little chopped parsley and simmer for
a few minutes. Pass through a sieve and season to taste. If
this sauce is to be kept warm, place in a double saucepan; it
should not cook any longer.

SALSA DE YEMAS DE HUEVO

Egg Yolk Sauce

4 Servings

1 oz. butter
1 oz. flour
2 egg yolks

1 cup stock
salt

Mix the butter and the flour over the fire, stirring for about
5 minutes, add the stock, bring to boil and take off the fire.
Beat egg yolks up and add together with a little more butter.
If this sauce is not served immediately put it into a double
saucepan and stir from time to time so that it does not
curdle.

SALSA DE TOMATE

Tomato Sauce

1 lb. fresh tomatoes or 1 tin
  tomatoes or tomato purée
1 chopped onion
1 garlic clove

1 teaspoon chopped parsley
salt and pepper
dash of sugar
fat or oil for frying

Fry the chopped onion, garlic clove and parsley till golden,
add the peeled tomatoes, simmer till the tomatoes have dis-
integrated, pass through a sieve and return to the fire to
simmer till sufficiently thick; season and add a dash of sugar
to take the acidity from the tomatoes.

SALSA ESPECIAL DE TOMATE

Special Tomato Sauce

2 lb. tomatoes or if tinned
  half the amount
3 onions
2 carrots
3 oz. butter, margarine
  or oil
1 tablespoon flour

1 garlic clove
1 teaspoon chopped parsley
bay leaf and thyme
salt and pepper
a little white wine
  (optional)

Heat the fat or oil in a saucepan, slightly fry the onions,
garlic and carrots. Gradually add the flour, stirring with a
wooden spoon so that it does not catch. Peel, cut up and add
the tomatoes, the parsley and the herbs, season and cover
the saucepan. Add a little white wine if desired. Leave on
a very low fire to simmer for 1 hour. Stir form time to time.
Pass through a sieve and return to the fire, till sufficiently
thick.

SALSA VERDE

Green Sauce

1 onion
1 tablespoon soft breadcrumbs
1 tablespoon chopped parsley
1 tablespoon capers
vinegar or white wine

1 chopped gherkin
3 anchovies
olive oil
1 lemon

Grate the onion and pound in a mortar together with the chopped parsley, the capers, chopped gherkin and anchovies. Continue pounding until a smooth paste is achieved, add the soft white breadcrumbs and continue to pound. Pour in a little oil (about 1 tablespoon) and mix well, then add the lemon juice. Dilute with a little vinegar or, even better, a little white wine.

SALSA ESPAÑOLA

Spanish Sauce

3 pints stock
4 oz. ham
4 oz. beef
1 glass sherry
1 pimento
salt and pepper

2 onions
2 tomatoes or 1 small tin
bay leaf
2 oz. butter
1 tablespoon chopped parsley
1 tablespoon flour

Melt the butter and gradually add the flour, stir with a wooden spoon, add the chopped onions, chopped parsley, bay leaf, pimento and stock. Put the beef and ham in and cook slowly for 2 hours. Add the sherry and the tomatoes. Simmer for a little while and serve hot.

SALSA PICANTE

Piquante Sauce

½ cup olive oil   1 grated onion
1 cup wine   2 grated garlic cloves
¼ cup vinegar   1 small dried red pepper
salt   a pinch of rosemary

Pound the onion, the garlic, rosemary, salt and red pepper to a paste, add the oil, mixing well. Mix the vinegar and wine (preferably red wine) and add. Allow to stand for a few hours. This makes a special salad dressing or a sauce for cold meat or chicken.

SALSA A LA AURORA

Aurora Sauce

½ cup béchamel (see p. 186)   ½ cup cream
½ cup stock   1 tablespoon finely
½ cup tomato juice   chopped ham

Put the béchamel, the tomato juice and the stock in a casserole and slowly bring to boil, take off the fire and whisk in the cream and the chopped ham. Serve hot.

SALSA VICTORIA

Victoria Sauce

3 tablespoons black-
  currant jelly
1 cup port or sherry
1 cup stock
1 orange

dash of cinnamon
salt and pepper
cayenne pepper
3 cloves

Melt the jelly over a low fire, add the port or sherry and the stock, the grated orange rind and the spices. Simmer for a little while and just before serving add the orange juice and a dash of cayenne pepper. This tasty sauce is excellent for duck and venison.

SALSA OSCURA

Dark Sauce

4 oz. lard or margarine
1 onion
1 carrot
1 tablespoon flour
bay leaf and marjoram

left-over meat or fowl
2 garlic cloves
a little red pepper
2 glasses red wine
1 pint stock

Fry the very finely chopped onion, carrot and garlic till golden, add the finely chopped cooked meat or fowl, the spices and stock. Mix flour with a little stock to a smooth paste and add to thicken the sauce. Simmer for about 30 minutes, add the wine, put through the sieve and serve boiled beef or venison.

SALSA VINAGRETA

Vinaigrette Sauce

oil	1 teaspoon capers
vinegar	1 teaspoon chopped parsley
salt and pepper	1 teaspoon chopped onion
1 hard-boiled egg	1 teaspoon chopped cucumber
pinch mustard	

The proportion of oil to vinegar is 3 spoonfuls oil to 1 of vinegar; if the vinegar proves too sour, add a little white wine. Mix the sauce up very well, add the finely chopped ingredients and season with salt, pepper and mustard. It is advisable to add the chopped egg at the last moment as it otherwise disintegrates. The sauce can also be made without the egg.

SALSA A LA MORNAY

Mornay Sauce

1 cup béchamel sauce (see p. 186)	2 tablespoons grated cheese
$\frac{1}{2}$ glass beer	cayenne pepper

Bring the beer to the boil and beat in the grated cheese. When it is well mixed, beat in the béchamel sauce. Continue to beat with a whisk for a few minutes and season with cayenne pepper. Serve hot.

SALSA CHAUD-FROID

Chaud-froid Sauce

There are quite a number of sauces that come under the category 'chaud-froid' and the story goes that a famous chef put a cold sauce on a hot dish, thus combining the hot and the cold. Pleased with the originality and success of this new experiment, he put hot sauces on a cold dish — it was still 'chaud-froid'. Here are the two most famous of these sauces:

CHAUD-FROID BLANCO

White Chaud-froid

½ pint good stock   1 glass white wine
¼ pint full cream   salt and pepper

Boil the stock with the wine for a few minutes, allow to cool and beat in the cream. Season. Serve with chicken or veal.

CHAUD-FROID VERDE

Green Chaud-froid

½ pint strong stock   ¼ pint full cream
1 cup spinach purée   salt and pepper
1 tablespoon capers   1 sour-sweet gherkin

Boil the capers, the gherkin and the spinach, season with salt and pepper and mash well together. Add the stock, put through a sieve and add the cream.

[193]

SALSA DE CARNE

Meat Sauce

4 oz. finely minced meat	$\frac{1}{2}$ glass wine
4 tomatoes or 1 tin purée	salt and pepper
1 chopped onion	a little oil or fat

Fry the finely chopped onion till golden, add the meat and fry till brown, dilute the tomato purée with the wine and a little water, add and slowly simmer for 30 minutes. This sauce can be passed through a sieve and served as a clear sauce. But with the meat it also makes a nice thick sauce for rice or spaghetti.

SALSA AMARILLA

Yellow Sauce

2 eggs	2 tablespoons oil
1 teaspoon French mustard	salt and pepper
1 tablespoon vinegar	

Mash the yolk of 1 hard-boiled egg, together with the mustard, and when smooth mix well with a raw yolk, beat up well and gradually add the oil and the vinegar, beating till the sauce thickens. Season and serve with salads, asparagus, etc. This sauce is delicious for potato salad.

SALSA DE PAN FRITO

Fried Bread Sauce

2 oz. breadcrumbs	2 tablespoons diced onion
1 cup stock or consommé	1 tablespoon chopped parsley
butter	juice of 1 lemon
2 tablespoons diced ham	

Fry the breadcrumbs and the onion, add the boiling stock with diced ham and parsley. Add the lemon juice. This sauce is nice with roast duck or chicken.

SALSA MUSELINA

White Wine Sauce

4 egg yolks	4 oz. butter
2 glasses white wine	juice of 1 lemon

Beat up the yolks, add the wine and simmer in a double saucepan. Melt the butter into this sauce, stirring all the while with a wooden spoon, then beat till frothy. Add the lemon juice and season. This sauce can be served with salt over chicken and rice or fish or with sugar over puddings.

SALSA MOSTAZA

Mustard Sauce

oz. butter	2 cups stock
½ oz. flour	2 tablespoons mustard
1 egg yolk	salt and pepper

Melt 1 oz. butter and stir in the flour to a smooth paste, add the stock and beat in the yolk. Mix the mustard with the rest of the butter and 1 tablespoon stock. Mix all together and serve hot. If this sauce has to be kept warm, put in a double saucepan, as it would otherwise thicken.

Postres

It is only on special occasions that a Spanish meal ends with any other dessert but cheese and fruit. There are many excellent cheeses in Spain, though little is exported. Much of it is goats' cheese, for these animals abound.

But at special times like birthdays, parties and also on Sundays the sweets are made with great care, very much sugar — and cream. It is not usual for much cake baking to be done at home — but the 'Pastelerias' have a wonderful selection for those with a sweet tooth. 'Borracho fino — despues del dulce vino' is what they say ('a connoisseur of wine drinks after the dessert').

One of the recipes you will find is for churros, which are simply crisply fried batter in the form of bars or sticks dipped in sugar. At every Fiesta and every Feria you will see the churrerias in

[197]

every town and village of Spain. These churros are delicious when eaten hot and the children and adults keep the churrero very busy forcing the batter through a funnel into the smoking oil.

SABAYON DE NARANJA

Orange Cream

6 Servings

2 oz. sugar
5 eggs
½ pint milk

½ pint orange juice with
juice of ½ lemon

Put the sugar in a double saucepan (bain-marie) beat up the yolks of 4 eggs together with the orange juice and add to the sugar. Beat 1 whole egg up with the milk and add. Beat all the time over the fire till it has turned into a thick, frothy cream.

POSTRE DE NARANJA

Orange Cup

4 Servings

4 oranges
½ pint orange juice
2 egg yolks
1 dessertspoon cornflour

4 oz. granulated sugar
¾ pint cream
4 candied cherries or peel

Cut the top off the oranges about a third of the way down, leaving a nice cup. Extract the flesh and juice. Blend cornflour with juice, add egg yolks and sugar. Beat over double saucepan (bain-marie) until it thickens. Pour into orange cups. Chill and decorate with whipped cream and candied peel.

CARAMEL CUSTARD

8 egg yolks
a few drops vanilla
    essence

1 pint milk
2 tablespoons syrup
4 oz. sugar

This is the most popular of all Spanish sweets and quite easy to make. Heat 3 tablespoons of sugar with $\frac{1}{2}$ tablespoon water till it is of a brown caramel consistency, pour into an oven-proof dish or little individual dishes, which have previously been dipped into cold water and not dried (this prevents sticking). Make a custard by beating the yolks well, adding the milk and the flavouring and pour into the caramel-lined dish or dishes and bake for about 20 minutes. Cool, turn out and keep in cool place till served.

MANZANAS RELLENAS

Stuffed Apples

6 Servings

6 large cooking apples
4 oz. sugar

2 eggs
2 tablespoons icing sugar

Scoop out the core and some of the flesh of the apples, sprinkle with a little sugar and put 2 tablespoons water in the pan so they do not catch. Bake until half done. In the meanwhile melt the sugar in 1 cup water till brown. Beat up the yolks and add. Pour this custard into the apples and bake in a medium hot oven till the custard has set. Beat the whites to a stiff snow, cover the apples with this and sprinkle with icing sugar. Put back in the oven till slightly golden and serve hot.

CREMA DE CHOCOLATE

Chocolate Cream

5 to 6 Servings

6 oz. plain chocolate
½ small cup black coffee
4 eggs

1 tablespoon rum or Curaçao
1 cup double cream
hazelnuts to decorate

Dissolve the chocolate in the hot coffee over a double sauce-pan (bain-marie). Take off the fire and beat in the egg yolks and the rum or liqueur. Beat up the whites, add the cream and beat till they are stiff and snowy; then fold in the chocolate and beat again. Pour into individual glasses, top with finely chopped hazelnuts and cool till served.

GRANIZADO DE CAFÉ

Coffee Sorbet

4 Servings

1 small pot black coffee
sugar

1 tablespoon Benedictine or
other sweet liqueur

Sweeten the coffee while it is hot. Allow to get cold, mix with the liqueur and pour into the freezing tray in your refrigerator. Allow to freeze, but not into one solid block. 1 hour will suffice. Beat up with a fork and serve in individual glasses.

BLANCO Y NEGRO

Black and White

As above, leaving room in the glass for a tablespoon of vanilla ice or frozen milk.

GRANIZADO DE LIMON

Lemon Sorbet

As coffee sorbet with lemon juice and sugar and a dash of syrup.

TORTILLA AL RON

Rum Omelette

4 Servings

6 eggs	rum
granulated sugar	butter
4 cubes sugar	salt

Beat up the egg yolks and separately beat up the whites till they are fairly stiff, then beat together with a pinch of salt. Put into hot buttered pan and shake so that the omelette does not stick. Fold on to a hot serving dish and sprinkle with sugar. On top place 4 cubes sugar. When on the table, pour the rum over the sugar till it almost dissolves. Set light to it and when the flame dies down, leaving a thick brown syrup on the omelette, serve.

CREMA DE MÁLAGA

Malaga Cream

5 Servings

12 egg yolks
4 glasses Malaga (or
sweet white wine)

6 oz. sugar
1 teaspoon cinnamon

Beat up the yolks till frothy, beat in the Malaga wine, together with the sugar and the cinnamon. Continue to beat over a low fire till the froth has risen considerably. Serve immediately in individual glasses.

BUÑUELOS DE MANZANA

Apple Fritters

6 Servings

9 oz. flour
3 eggs
3 tablespoons sugar
¼ pint milk

1 coffeespoon baking powder
icing sugar
1 lb. large apples
fat for frying

Peel and core the apples, cut into thick slices. Make a batter with the flour, yolks, sugar, baking powder and milk, fold in the beaten egg whites. Dip the apple slices in the batter and deep fry. Sprinkle with icing sugar and serve hot.

BUDÍN PORTORRIQUEÑO

Puerto Rican Pudding

stale white bread or stale
   sponge cake
milk
1 oz. butter
sugar
1 teaspoon cinnamon

3 cloves
toasted almonds
raisins
2 glasses white wine
2 eggs

Soak the bread or cake in milk and wine till soft, beat up
with sufficient sugar to taste. Beat up eggs and add, together
with butter, cinnamon and cloves. Soak the raisins in wine,
take the pips out and add, together with the wine. Beat
everything well together and put into a greased pudding
basin. Sprinkle with toasted almonds and butter the top.
Bake in the oven till golden.

TARTA VALENCIANA

Valencia Pudding

4 Servings

3 eggs
5 oz. sugar
4 oz. toasted almonds
   (ground)

8 oz. boiled, mashed
   potatoes
1½ tablespoons butter

Beat the egg yolks with the sugar, mix with the potato purée
and ground almonds and knead to a dough. Beat the whites
to a stiff snow and fold in. Pour the batter into a greased
baking dish and bake in a very hot oven for 10—15 minutes.

VISITAS

Little Cakes for Visitors

2 Dozen

7 oz. icing sugar	2½ oz. ground almonds
3½ oz. flour	4 egg whites
3 oz. butter	sugar for caramel

Cream the butter and add the sugar. Beat the whites to stiff snow and fold in, heat well and add the ground almonds and the flour. Bake in individual shapes or paper cups in a moderate oven. When cold, glaze with caramel (boiled sugar).

BIZCOCHO DE ALMENDRA

Almond Cake

½ oz. butter	3 oz. biscuit crumbs
5 oz. sugar	6 eggs
5 oz. ground almonds	

Beat the yolks with the sugar till firm and frothy. Beat the whites to a stiff snow and fold in. Add the biscuit crumbs and ground almonds and beat well. Pour the mixture into a well buttered baking tin and bake in a moderate oven for 15 minutes.

BORRACHITOS

Tipsy Cakes

3½ oz. butter
2 oz. sugar
1 teaspoon vanilla essence

3 eggs
5 oz. flour
1 teaspoon baking powder
sugar to glaze

Cream the butter with the sugar, add the vanilla essence. Beat up the yolks and mix with the flour and baking powder. Beat up the whites to snow and add, mixing well. Pour the batter into small greased tins or paper cups. Bake in a hot oven. Allow to cool and pour melted sugar syrup over them.

BUÑUELITOS DE SAN JOSÉ

St. Joseph's Day Fritters

4 oz. rice
1 pint milk
vanilla or vanilla essence
1 glass sweet sherry
1 lemon

3 eggs
2 oz. flour
breadcrumbs
fat or oil for frying
icing sugar

Boil the rice in sweetened milk and vanilla for about 20 minutes, when it should be tender and have absorbed all the milk. Flavour with grated lemon rind. When cool, beat in 2 whole eggs, the juice of ½ lemon and the flour. Add sweet sherry. Mix well and leave for several hours in a cool place, preferably the refrigerator. Roll into little balls or croquettes. Baste in beaten egg and breadcrumbs and deep fry in hot fat or oil. Drain well and sprinkle with icing sugar.

BIZCOCHOS DE AVELLANA

Hazelnut Biscuits

8 oz. ground hazelnuts	1 tablespoon grated lemon rind
1 egg	juice of $\frac{1}{2}$ lemon
2 oz. flour	3 oz. castor sugar

Pound the hazelnuts with the sugar in a mortar to a fine paste, add the flour and lemon rind. Beat the egg and lemon juice together and add to the mixture, place teaspoonfuls on a greased baking sheet and bake in a moderate oven until the little biscuits are brown and crisp.

MELOCOTONES EN ALMIBAR

Peaches in Syrup

6 Servings

1 large tin peaches in syrup	2 glasses sherry or sweet
6 slices sponge or fruit cake	wine
strawberry jam	hazelnuts or candied peel
$\frac{1}{4}$ pint cream	to decorate

Take individual dessert cups or dishes. At the bottom of each place a piece of sponge or fruit cake and soak well in sherry, mixed with a little juice of the peaches. On this place several halves of peaches. Over these spread a layer of strawberry jam. Whip up the cream and fill the glasses. Sprinkle with a little chopped hazelnut or candied peel.

CHURROS

Fried Batter

½ pint water	2 eggs
1 oz. butter	fat or oil for frying
8 oz. flour	sugar
pinch salt	icing sugar

Put the water into a large saucepan and when warm add the butter, a pinch of salt and a little sugar. Stir and when it comes to the boil carefully add the flour, stirring all the time with a wooden spoon to a smooth batter. Remove from the fire and beat in the eggs, stir till smooth. Heat the oil till it smokes, force the mixture through a funnel into the hot oil and deep fry till golden. Cut the churros with scissors into sticks and drain. Sprinkle with icing sugar and eat hot or cold.

Churros at the fairs and in the street 'churrerias' are usually made without egg.

SOUFLÉ FRIO DE FRESA

Cold Strawberry Soufflé

4 Servings

6 oz. strawberries	1 dessertspoon Kirsch
3 heaped dessertspoons castor sugar	3 egg whites
	greased soufflé mould

Whisk the egg whites until very stiff. Sieve the strawberries and stir with the sugar and Kirsch. Fold the egg whites into this mixture and beat gently until blended. Tip into the buttered mould. Bake for 3½ minutes in a moderate oven (Regulo 5—6). This soufflé should not drop when cold.

TORTA DE MIEL Y NUECES

Honey and Nut Roll

8 oz. flour	1 egg
4 oz. butter	½ glass sherry
pinch of salt	chopped walnuts
honey	and hazelnuts
1 tablespoon	juice of ½ lemon
castor sugar	

Make a rich short pastry as follows. Rub the butter into the
flour, add salt and castor sugar. Add the beaten egg yolk,
lemon juice and sherry to make into a stiff paste. If necessary
add a little cold water. Roll into a strip. Brush with honey
and sprinkle with the chopped nuts (chopped candied peel
can also be added). Roll and sprinkle with a little more castor
sugar. Bake in a moderate oven for about 20 minutes.

PASTELITOS DE MIEL

Honey Fritters

8 oz. flour	1 coffeespoon baking
3 tablespoons sweet wine	powder
2 eggs	oil for frying
3 tablespoons sugar	honey

Pour the flour onto the table leaving a well in the centre for
the beaten eggs, sugar and baking powder. Mix these ingredients well into the flour, add wine and knead into a smooth
dough. Roll out fine and cut into 3-inch strips about 1 inch
wide. Deep fry these biscuits, drain well and dip into honey.
Leave to cool.

TORTA DE QUESO

Spanish Cheese Cake

short pastry (see p. 77)
3 eggs
4 oz. sugar
vanilla essence

1 lb. cottage cheese
1 tablespoon candied peel
icing sugar
2 tablespoons seedless
  raisins

Beat the eggs till they are frothy, separately whisk the cheese until creamy and mix, add vanilla essence and the sugar. Beat everything well together and finally add the seedless raisins and chopped peel. Grease a cake dish, line with the short pastry and fill with the mixture. Bake in a very hot oven for about 10 minutes, then reduce the heat to moderate and continue to bake for about 20 minutes until the cheese filling has set. When done leave inside the open oven to cool gradually. Serve when cold.

CREMA ITALIANA

Italian Cream

12 egg yolks
4 glasses of Malaga wine
  (or sweet white wine)

6 oz. sugar
a little cinnamon

Beat the eggs till frothy with a whisk. Beat in the wine, the sugar and cinnamon. Put in a casserole over a low fire, beating all the time till it is a thick, frothy cream. Serve immediately in individual glasses.

PLATANOS A LA PORTORRIQUEÑO

Bananas Puerto Rican Style

bananas	cinnamon
white wine	oil for frying
sugar	

Peel and fry the bananas till golden. Add some white wine, sugar and cinnamon. Simmer for a few moments and serve hot.

JEREZ

Sherry

No book on Spanish cooking would be complete without a mention of sherry - and what better way of ending a Spanish meal than with one of the rich, sweet varieties?

Sherry is made from the white grapes that grow in the south of Spain. The name is taken from the Andalusian town of Jerez, the centre of the sherry distilleries. There are many wines called sherry, but there is no other wine in the world quite like the real *Jerez*, which is made from the very best of the good wine of each vintage and kept for many years to mature in huge barrels to blend with the best wines from other years. There is the dry sherry, which is of a pale amber colour, the medium dry which is slightly darker and the very sweet which is dark and rich and is termed Oloroso or Amoroso.

And the Spanish toast is: SALUD Y PESETAS!

INDEX OF RECIPES

Printed in Czechoslovakia